Aid to Africa

Other Books in the Current Controversies Series

CONTROVERSIES

Aid to Africa

Debra A. Miller, Book Editor

GREENHAVEN PRESS
A part of Gale, Cengage Learning

GALE
CENGAGE Learning™

Detroit • New York • San Francisco • New Haven, Conn • Waterville, Maine • London

GALE
CENGAGE Learning

Christine Nasso, *Publisher*
Elizabeth Des Chenes, *Managing Editor*

© 2009 Greenhaven Press, a part of Gale, Cengage Learning

Gale and Greenhaven Press are registered trademarks used herein under license.

For more information, contact:
Greenhaven Press
27500 Drake Rd.
Farmington Hills, MI 48331-3535
Or you can visit our Internet site at gale.cengage.com

For product information and technology assistance, contact us at

Gale Customer Support, 1-800-877-4253
For permission to use material from this text or product, submit all requests online at www.cengage.com/permissions

Further permissions questions can be emailed to permissionrequest@cengage.com

Articles in Greenhaven Press anthologies are often edited for length to meet page requirements. In addition, original titles of these works are changed to clearly present the main thesis and to explicitly indicate the author's opinion. Every effort is made to ensure that Greenhaven Press accurately reflects the original intent of the authors. Every effort has been made to trace the owners of copyrighted material.

Cover image © Peter Turnley/Corbis.

LIBRARY OF CONGRESS CATALOGING-IN-PUBLICATION DATA

Aid to Africa / Debra A. Miller, book editor.
 p. cm. -- (Current controversies)
 Includes bibliographical references and index.
 ISBN 978-0-7377-4316-6 (hardcover)
 ISBN 978-0-7377-4315-9 (pbk.)
 1. Economic assistance--Africa. 2. Poverty--Africa. 3. Africa--Commerce. 4. Economic development--Africa. I. Miller, Debra A.
 HC800.Z9P63174 2009
 338.91096--dc22
                                                                2008043434

Printed in the United States of America
1 2 3 4 5 6 7 13 12 11 10 09

Contents

Chapter 3: Will Trade Benefit African Nations?

Chapter 4: Will Oil and Other Natural Resources Save Africa?

Foreword

By definition, controversies are "discussions of questions in which opposing opinions clash" (Webster's Twentieth Century Dictionary Unabridged). Few would deny that controversies are a pervasive part of the human condition and exist on virtually every level of human enterprise. Controversies transpire between individuals and among groups, within nations and between nations. Controversies supply the grist necessary for progress by providing challenges and challengers to the status quo. They also create atmospheres where strife and warfare can flourish. A world without controversies would be a peaceful world; but it also would be, by and large, static and prosaic.

The Series' Purpose

The purpose of the *Current Controversies* series is to explore many of the social, political, and economic controversies dominating the national and international scenes today. Titles selected for inclusion in the series are highly focused and specific. For example, from the larger category of criminal justice, *Current Controversies* deals with specific topics such as police brutality, gun control, white collar crime, and others. The debates in *Current Controversies* also are presented in a useful, timeless fashion. Articles and book excerpts included in each title are selected if they contribute valuable, long-range ideas to the overall debate. And wherever possible, current information is enhanced with historical documents and other relevant materials. Thus, while individual titles are current in focus, every effort is made to ensure that they will not become quickly outdated. Books in the *Current Controversies* series will remain important resources for librarians, teachers, and students for many years.

In addition to keeping the titles focused and specific, great care is taken in the editorial format of each book in the series. Book introductions and chapter prefaces are offered to provide background material for readers. Chapters are organized around several key questions that are answered with diverse opinions representing all points on the political spectrum. Materials in each chapter include opinions in which authors clearly disagree as well as alternative opinions in which authors may agree on a broader issue but disagree on the possible solutions. In this way, the content of each volume in *Current Controversies* mirrors the mosaic of opinions encountered in society. Readers will quickly realize that there are many viable answers to these complex issues. By questioning each author's conclusions, students and casual readers can begin to develop the critical thinking skills so important to evaluating opinionated material.

Current Controversies is also ideal for controlled research. Each anthology in the series is composed of primary sources taken from a wide gamut of informational categories including periodicals, newspapers, books, U.S. and foreign government documents, and the publications of private and public organizations. Readers will find factual support for reports, debates, and research papers covering all areas of important issues. In addition, an annotated table of contents, an index, a book and periodical bibliography, and a list of organizations to contact are included in each book to expedite further research.

Perhaps more than ever before in history, people are confronted with diverse and contradictory information. During the Persian Gulf War, for example, the public was not only treated to minute-to-minute coverage of the war, it was also inundated with critiques of the coverage and countless analyses of the factors motivating U.S. involvement. Being able to sort through the plethora of opinions accompanying today's major issues, and to draw one's own conclusions, can be a complicated and frustrating struggle. It is the editors' hope that *Current Controversies* will help readers with this struggle.

Introduction

"Although often portrayed as a place of poverty and despair, Africa is also an incredibly rich and diverse part of the world."

Although often portrayed as a place of poverty and despair, Africa is also an incredibly rich and diverse part of the world. It is one of the world's largest and most populated continents, second only to Asia in both categories. Lying across the equator, Africa is so large that it stretches into four hemispheres—running about 5,000 miles (8,047 km) from north to south and 4,700 miles (7,564 km) east to west. And with a fast-growing population of more than 900 million people, Africa makes up more than 14 percent of the global human population.

Africa is also a land of great geographical and biological diversity. Much of northern Africa is arid and covered by the Sahara Desert—a vast area of gravel, rock, and shifting sands. In contrast, the region south of the Sahara—called sub-Sahara—is tropical and features rain forests, massive river systems, grasslands, islands, and beaches. And although most of Africa's interior is a wide, low-lying plateau, the continent also has numerous volcanoes, including Africa's highest peak— Mount Kilimanjaro (19,340 feet/5,895 m). Africa's greatest wealth, however, lies in its remarkable biodiversity, which includes not only rich, untapped mineral and oil resources and great natural beauty, but also exotic animals such as gorillas, chimpanzees, zebras, giraffes, hippopotamuses, and elephants.

Africa is home to fifty-three independent countries that vary widely in size and economic development, and each African country is a mix of tribes with many unique languages and cultures. Of Africa's five geographical regions, Southern

Africa is the most economically developed. It is home to ten countries—South Africa, Angola, Botswana, Lesotho, Malawi, Mozambique, Namibia, Swaziland, Zambia and Zimbabwe. Angola has recently begun to thrive economically due to oil discoveries, but the Republic of South Africa, a nation situated at the very southern tip of the continent, has long been the economic and political leader of the region. Once colonized by both the Dutch and the British, South Africa became independent in 1961 but lived under a rigid system of apartheid (racial segregation) until 1990. Democratic elections were held in 1994, and, since then, South Africa's economy has grown rapidly. Although still fighting poverty and other problems common to the rest of the continent, the country today is a center for mining, oil and gas production, chemical manufacturing, agriculture, tourism, and trade.

The region of North Africa, which lies north of the Sahara Desert, is the second-most developed region of Africa and is made up of five Muslim nations—Egypt, Libya, Tunisia, Algeria, and Morocco. This part of the continent borders the southern shore of the Mediterranean Sea, and although once colonized as part of European spice trade routes, it now identifies strongly with the Arab world. Some of these countries have experienced high economic growth in recent years. Both Algeria and Libya, for example, have large oil and gas reserves and are active members of the Organization of Petroleum Exporting Countries (OPEC), which controls the price of much of the world's oil. At the same time, this region has become increasingly prone to the Islamic terrorist violence that has afflicted the Middle East. Algeria, for example, has been the site of decades of violence—first a war for independence from France in 1962 and most recently a prolonged power struggle between Islamic militants and the country's military.

West Africa is a region bordering the Atlantic Ocean that is divided into seventeen different countries—Benin, Burkina Faso, Cameroon, Cape Verde, Côte d'Ivoire, Gambia, Ghana,

Guinea, Guinea-Bissau, Liberia, Mali, Mauritania, Niger, Nigeria, Senegal, Sierra Leone, and Togo. Countries here (except for Liberia) were colonized by Britain and France and today are divided into French- and English-speaking states. By 1974, all of these nations had achieved independence, but since then most have struggled with political instability and have failed to manage natural resources to benefit local economies. Nigeria, for example, is awash in oil and is a major U.S. trading partner, but the nation is still plagued by poverty, disease, ethnic and religious violence, and government corruption. Liberia, too, has ties to the United States; it was founded by descendants of American slaves who returned to Africa. It, however, has also been torn apart by years of internal strife. Both Nigeria and Liberia have recently elected civilian leaders, so there is hope that these new democracies will be able to create a more prosperous and peaceful future.

East Africa comprises a strip of fourteen countries along Africa's eastern coast—Eritrea, Ethiopia, Somalia, and Djibouti (all located in the part of Africa that juts out into the Indian Ocean known as the Horn of Africa), Sudan, Uganda, Kenya, Tanzania, Rwanda, and Burundi on the mainland, and several small island states: the Comoros, Mauritius, the Seychelles, and Madagascar. These areas also once lived under European rule and now share problems of low economic development and a history of military coups, political corruption, and violence. Kenya and Tanzania, known for their large wildlife reserves, have had the most stable governments. Kenya is also the most economically developed country in the region, although its economic success has been threatened since 2007 by a new episode of political unrest.

Central Africa lies in the tropical heart of the continent, with a few states bordering the southern Atlantic coast, and comprises seven countries—the Central African Republic, Chad, Congo, the Democratic Republic of Congo, Equatorial Guinea, Gabon, São Tomé, and Príncipe. This region is dominated by the powerful Congo River and its large, biologically rich rain forest basin. Its industries include crops such as cocoa, coffee, and rubber, plus fishing and logging. The last part of the continent to be colonized, it also fell under European control in the late nineteenth century. The largest country here is the Democratic Republic of Congo (DRC), covering much of the African interior. The DRC achieved its independence in 1960 but was ruled by a corrupt, U.S.-supported dictator until 1997, when the country slid into violence and war. Today, even after democratic elections, the DRC remains unstable, and like many other African nations, it is backward economically with a high incidence of poverty and disease.

Commentators often attribute Africa's problems of poverty and lack of development to the legacy of European colonial rule. Although the Europeans introduced industries such as mining and commercial farming, colonialism left many African countries dependent on the export of just one or two products and placed them at the mercy of world price fluctuations. Independence, however, did not correct these economic problems but instead ushered in numerous inept, corrupt African leaders. Over the last fifty years, to help poor Africans, the developed world has distributed $2.3 trillion in aid, yet poverty and chronic underdevelopment persist. This situation has created a debate over the value of foreign aid, with some analysts claiming that more aid is needed and others arguing that aid has hurt Africa by making it economically dependent. The authors in *Current Controversies: Aid to Africa* highlight some of the difficult problems facing Africa and debate whether aid, increased trade, or future exploitation of oil and other natural resources might provide a solution to Africa's ills.

CHAPTER 1

What Problems Are Facing Africa?

Chapter Preface

Although Africa faces many developmental challenges, one of the most formidable problems is a lack of information and communication technologies (ICT) such as telephone lines, radios, television sets, computers, and Internet connections. The gap between people with access to ICT and those without is often referred to as the "digital divide."

In Africa, the digital divide is quite extreme. In fact, Africa has the fewest ICT tools of any region in the world. Out of a population of about 963 million people, only a tiny minority has access to a computer, a telephone, a television set, or even a radio. The problem is even worse in rural areas, where the majority of Africans live, and where a lack of infrastructure—such as roads, telephone lines, and electricity—prevents almost all types of electronic communication. The contrast between these rural Africans and most of the rest of the world is striking: In an age when many people in other regions can communicate instantly and globally using wireless and satellite technologies, most people in Africa cannot even dream of making a simple telephone call to their neighbors.

Africa's lack of infrastructure is the biggest obstacle to telecommunications expansion, but other challenges involve overcoming the significant differences in public policies, regulatory frameworks, and wealth distribution of Africa's various countries. Today, there remain major disparities among African nations; 75 percent of the continent's fixed telephone lines, for example, are located in just six of Africa's fifty-three countries.

This digital divide in Africa isolates the continent from the rest of the world and makes it nearly impossible for Africans to trade effectively with other nations. In today's world, businesses from around the world share information instantly through ICT networks, creating a global economy. Those who cannot participate in those networks lose market opportunities and cannot hope to be globally competitive. Developing these ICT links has been shown to boost local economies and fuel economic growth and employment.

Although it is still technologically backward, Africa has made great strides in recent years toward improving its telecommunications capabilities. Between 1995 and 2001, for example, the number of land telephone lines increased from 12.5 million to 21 million. Many areas also saw an increase in the number of public phone booths and community communications centers, where people share telephones and televisions. Today, wireless technologies and mobile phones are fast becoming the main method of communication. The number of cell phone users doubles every year, and they now outnumber fixed-line phones on the continent. Africa has about 280 million total telephone subscribers, and over 85 percent, or about 260 million, of these are mobile subscribers. In fact, Africa has become the fastest growing cellular phone market in the world.

Africa also has increased its Internet usage, but in this area it remains far behind the developed world. Only about 5 percent of Africans have Internet access; this translates into approximately 50 million Internet users. By comparison, Europe's Internet penetration is eight times larger. And broadband, a technology that allows the transmittal of much larger amounts of data and information than telephone lines, has only begun to be available in Africa. In developed countries, broadband is now available to more than 18 percent of these populations.

For the minority of fortunate Africans with access to these new information technologies, life is changing for the better. Some rural farmers, for example, are now able to get real-time information on market prices for their produce using cell phones. Some entrepreneurs who once had to use land telephone lines to do business now can connect with suppliers and customers via Web sites and the Internet. And a few teachers and local broadcasters are also using the Internet to access educational information, news, and music that can then be redistributed in local communities.

Despite the clear challenges involved, many experts say Africa presents an attractive market for telecommunication investors. Already, many African governments have begun to prioritize ICT development, and they are getting help from large ICT companies who stand to gain if Africa can be brought into the digital world. One example of these partnerships is the Connect Africa initiative—a group of African leaders and representatives from various global ICT corporations who met in 2007 to develop a plan to bridge ICT infrastructure gaps on the continent.

The digital divide, however, may be the least-pressing issue on Africa's agenda because the region is coping with more dire problems, among them extreme poverty, hunger, disease, and rampant government corruption. The viewpoints in this chapter identify some of the many challenges facing the continent.

AIDS Still Plagues Africa

Craig Timberg

Craig Timberg is a staff writer for The Washington Post, *a daily U.S. newspaper based in Washington, D.C.*

Five years after President [George W.] Bush vowed to "turn the tide against AIDS" in Africa he is traveling across a continent where the government's $15 billion investment has extended the lives of hundreds of thousands of people and eased the sense of certain doom once experienced by millions of others.

But in the worst-hit areas, clustered mainly on Africa's southern tip, the tide has decidedly not turned. The epidemic continues to spread at a torrid pace that shows little sign of easing, with people contracting HIV much faster than sick ones can be put on crucial antiretroviral drugs, research shows.

The Bush AIDS Initiative

Bush's initiative, the President's Emergency Program for AIDS Relief, or PEPFAR, has not found a way to prevent a significant number of the estimated 1.7 million new cases of HIV each year in Africa. Nearly half of today's 15-year-olds in South Africa, one of the biggest beneficiaries of the program, will contract the virus in their lifetimes at current infection rates, estimates show.

Prevention messages . . . continue to stress condoms, HIV testing and abstinence—none of which have demonstrated major impacts in slowing the AIDS epidemic in Africa.

"They've turned the treatment tide in a fundamental way," said François Venter, president of the Southern African HIV

Craig Timberg, "African AIDS Crisis Outlives $15 Billion Bush Initiative," *The Washington Post*, February 20, 2008, p. A09. Reprinted with permission.

Clinicians Society, who works on several programs that receive PEPFAR funding, referring to administration officials. "In terms of prevention, they haven't. . . . It's quite clear that [South Africa's] prevention programs have failed completely."

In southern Africa's increasingly plentiful and well-funded AIDS clinics, patients appear healthy as they get checkups and pick up monthly supplies of antiretroviral drugs. But prevention messages, inside the clinics and beyond, continue to stress condoms, HIV testing and abstinence—none of which have demonstrated major impacts in slowing the AIDS epidemic in Africa.

Interventions that research shows can slow the epidemic, such as circumcising men, encouraging monogamy and making contraception widely available to infected women, have gained relatively little attention. And new technologies, such as vaccines and vaginal microbicides, have continued to disappoint in research trials despite massive investments.

Bush announced PEPFAR in his 2003 State of the Union address, promising to prevent 7 million new infections while treating at least 2 million people with antiretroviral drugs. "I ask the Congress to commit $15 billion over the next five years, including nearly $10 billion in new money, to turn the tide against AIDS in the most afflicted nations of Africa and the Carribbean. This nation can lead the world in sparing innocent people from a plague of nature," Bush said.

The money is heavily weighted toward 15 "focus countries," 12 of which are in Africa. As the initial investment nears its end, Bush has called for renewing the program at double the original amount over the next five years. The two leading Democratic candidates are urging even more.

Winning Over Skeptics

PEPFAR has won over some skeptics, including Paul Farmer, a founder of Partners in Health, a Boston nonprofit that provides medical services in Africa and elsewhere. "As someone who has been highly critical of [the Bush] administration's foreign policies, PEPFAR and other investments in health have outstripped that of all other administrations," said Farmer, who works extensively in Rwanda, where Bush was [in February 2008].

It also has impressed Eric Goemaere, the top official in South Africa for Doctors Without Borders, which initially criticized Bush for resisting the use of generic drugs and failing to integrate its AIDS effort with national health programs. "Five years down the line, they have been much more promising than many other funders," Goemaere said. Bush's treatment goal appears on track. The White House says that PEPFAR is supporting the treatment of 1.3 million Africans, though in some cases that support is indirect, such as formulating policies or improving management systems for national health programs that would have been treating their citizens anyway. Also, research suggests that 40 percent of Africans who start on antiretroviral drugs cannot be accounted for two years later because they stopped taking the medicine, transferred to another program or died.

Venter said the infusion of money from PEPFAR enabled two clinics he helps oversee to offer more drugs to more people by improving the training of nurses, providing medical tests and paying some staff salaries. One of the clinics, Venter said, used to add about 10 people a month to its roster of patients on antiretroviral drugs; now that number exceeds 150. "That's happened with a lot of effort, and that's largely on account of the PEPFAR program," Venter said.

Problems with Prevention

On prevention, the officials who implement PEPFAR have largely abandoned its most audacious and specific claims. Instead they tabulate how many people, for example, may have heard a radio show on AIDS, without attempting to estimate how many avoided contracting HIV as a result.

They do claim, however, to have helped prevent 157,000 cases of pediatric HIV by assisting programs that have provided antiretroviral drugs to pregnant women. Administration officials rarely mention, however, that they have resisted calls to provide women with contraceptives.

Studies have shown that family planning could avert far more infections than antiretroviral drugs because many women, especially those with HIV, want fewer children. Critics say the restriction, along with PEPFAR's emphasis on untested abstinence programs, exists mainly to win support from conservative congressional Republicans, undermining the full potential of a program that the White House bills as one of the biggest humanitarian ventures in history.

The AIDS epidemic can be contained by forces other than U.S. money and political will.

"The same money spent in more evidence-based ways would bring more health and happiness," said Malcolm Potts, former head of Family Health International, a research group that receives significant PEPFAR funding.

But PEPFAR officials have adapted. After initial reluctance, they have begun supporting efforts to offer circumcision services for men, which three major experiments in Africa have shown could slow infection rates by more than 60 percent.

The program has also branched out beyond AIDS, which in most African nations kills fewer people than does malaria, malnutrition or contaminated water. In Rwanda, the 3 percent HIV rate is far lower than in southern African nations. PEPFAR money increasingly is used to improve basic medical services.

Yet the past five years have also shown that the AIDS epidemic can be contained by forces other than U.S. money and political will. Africa's biggest declines in HIV rates during Bush's AIDS initiative have come in Zimbabwe, where economic collapse has coincided with fundamental social change, including a shift toward monogamy and away from more-costly multiple relationships, research there shows.

The changes have come as [Zimbabwe] President Robert Mugabe's ruinous rule has driven away foreign funding. Each of its neighbors—which all lag behind Zimbabwe in slowing HIV—are PEPFAR focus countries. Zimbabwe is not.

Soaring Energy Prices Prevent Economic Development in Africa

Rebecca Schultz

Rebecca Schultz is a research associate on the national security team at the Center for American Progress, a progressive think tank in Washington, D.C.

With world crude oil prices ... [rising], economies across Africa are grinding to a halt under the burden of soaring energy costs. The spike in world oil prices ... will exacerbate economic problems, pounding already fragile national budgets and offsetting hard-fought gains from poverty reduction programs, international development aid, and debt relief efforts.

High oil prices slam the door on prospects for economic development in poor countries. The poorest of the poor will not feel the immediate effects—the 747 million Africans who still use firewood and dung to cook their meals, don't have access to electricity, don't take shared taxis to market, and don't have motorcycles to fill up with gas. But the urban poor and working classes who are just high enough up the economic ladder to marginally benefit from basic modern services and transportation will be bitterly squeezed by rising oil prices.

Africa's hardworking urban poor are almost always creatively productive as they strive to better their lives and those of their families. Countries across the continent pin their hopes on the upward mobility of the urban poor—a hope shared around the globe, in fact, for a more secure and equitable world tomorrow. Alas, those African countries not af-

Rebecca Schultz, "Africa's Energy Crisis Worsens: Viable Clean Energy Alternatives Are Imperative," Center for American Progress, July 17, 2007. Reproduced by permission. This material was created for the Progress Report, the daily e-mail publication of the Center for American Progress. You can sign up online at www.progressreport.org.

flicted by the "curse of oil," such as Nigeria, Gabon, Sudan, Algeria and Libya, are plagued by the cost of rising global oil prices. . . . [Summer of 2007] brings another season of skyrocketing oil prices, which means already struggling economies in Africa may well shut down under additional cost burdens. As long as clean energy alternatives are absent in these countries, hard-won achievements in economic development will continue to fall prey to oil prices. Africa has plenty of opportunities to exploit renewable energy resources such as wind, solar, and geothermal power. And renewable biofuels production is equally promising.

The United States must take the lead on making clean energy in Africa a priority for the international community and work with developing countries to help them leapfrog the oil dependence that holds advanced industrial economies hostage today. The 21st century will indisputably be characterized by global interdependence, shared risks, and shared benefits. There are millions of people in Africa with stunted economic horizons, without functioning school systems and hospitals, and frustrated by their governments' spending money on oil instead of basic human services—problems that pose a threat to the interests of global security, the magnitude of which the United States and its allies have only just begun to appreciate.

The Crisis in West Africa

In Senegal's capital city of Dakar, the cost of taxis has almost doubled since 2005 and blackouts occurred every day [in the summer of 2006] because the state-owned utilities couldn't afford to pay for fuel. The country relies on oil imports to power its diesel-fired generators, and while conditions relaxed somewhat over the winter, power cuts are on the rise again. As of May [2007], the capital was facing 10-hour power cuts several times a week and the government was warning of impending, unprecedented shortages.

Senegal is paying nearly twice what it was a few years ago to import the same amount of oil. The increased cost alone is more than seven times as much as the country is gaining through multilateral debt relief programs. The government has responded to the energy crisis by providing direct subsidies to consumers. Since the rise in world oil prices began in 2002, these subsidies have increased five-fold, creating yet another incredible burden on the national budget.

Muslim Senegal is one of West Africa's most stable democracies, and until recently had been considered one of the few countries where the Millennium Development Goals—a set of goals such as achieving universal primary education, which were adopted by the world's governments as a roadmap for reducing poverty—could have been achieved by the 2015 target date. But those prospects are looking increasingly grim these days. Even excluding domestic support mechanisms, Senegal spends about the same amount on health and education combined as it does importing oil, roughly 8.5 percent of its gross domestic product [GDP].

Similar trends are occurring elsewhere in Africa, where scarce budgetary resources, desperately needed in the health and education sectors, are being spent to cushion oil and electricity costs. Indeed, Senegal's West African neighbors are even worse off.

Guinea, Guinea Bissau, and the Gambia—all of which, like Senegal, are dependent on imports for 100 percent of the oil that they consume—spend a fraction of the amount of their oil bills on public services and poverty reduction expenditures. The gains of debt relief accumulated over the last decade are fast being wiped out, and annual debt savings today are grossly overshadowed by the unprecedented drain on their budgets due to record oil prices.

The Crisis in East Africa

The problem goes beyond West Africa. Take Uganda in the great lakes region of East Africa, one of the poorest countries in the world. Years of steady economic growth and a population explosion—Uganda has the highest population growth rate in Africa—have combined to create an energy crisis when not long ago the country was exporting its surplus electricity to neighbors.

Uganda has been plagued by increasingly frequent and severe power outages from its hydroelectric stations on the upper tributaries of the Nile River flowing in and out of Lake Victoria. Due in part to global warming, the water levels of Lake Victoria, the largest of Africa's great lakes, have been decreasing steadily over the last decade.

With regional droughts, water levels dropped an astonishing half an inch per day in most of 2006. Uganda's use of clean, renewable hydroelectric energy has served well to diversify the country's fuel-mix and shield the economy from volatile world oil markets, but river flow and water levels are so low today that the dams are generating power at one-third of capacity.

Last fall [2006], Uganda experienced one of the worst power shortages in its history. The government resorted to an extreme load-shedding regimen, providing power only every other day. Responding to the emergency with the support of the World Bank, it installed two diesel-fired generators to relieve the shortage—a less-than-perfect solution for numerous reasons. The generators are energy-intensive. They emit high concentrations of greenhouse gases. They require that oil be imported (modest oil reserves were recently discovered in western Uganda, but are not online). And, not least, they produce power at significantly higher cost than the hydroelectric generators.

The bill for importing the fuel to power these plants amounts to roughly $150 million per year, a cost the government subsidizes and then rolls off to consumers, who in turn have seen their electricity bills double in the last year. To keep this in perspective, the average Ugandan makes around $280 per year, but pays $5.50 per gallon at the pump and an average 24 cents per kilowatt hour [kWh] for electricity, as compared to eight cents per kWh in the United States.

In the meantime, these two generators have led to a rapid escalation in the demand for diesel, causing widespread fuel shortages across Uganda's capital city of Kampala. When they are delivered, diesel supplies at Kampala fueling stations last less than 24 hours before selling out. Now, when the national power grid cuts the power supply, which still happens for extended periods at a time, businesses that had come to rely on their own back-up generators can't find the diesel to run them.

The poorest countries in the world consume an almost negligible share of the . . . [world's] oil . . . , yet they are hit the most by rising world oil prices.

From small enterprises to manufacturing factories, business across the country have been forced to lay off workers and shut down operations. The government has approximated that power shortages [in 2006] cost the economy $250 million, but that is likely a low-ball figure. [In 2007] the situation could be just as bad if not worse. Diesel shortages are still wide-spread and black-outs are leaving the capital dark for up to 30 hours at a time.

East Africa may be less dependent on oil than other parts of the continent due to its considerable hydropower capacity, but even that buffer is fast eroding. Across Lake Victoria from Uganda, Tanzania is another country that suffered a similar fate in 2006, its worst power failure in decades.

Tanzania's commercial fuel-mix is relatively diversified, and the country generates more hydroelectricity than any other country in the region. Yet severe drought [in 2006] caused such a reduction in electricity supplies that the country was forced to revise its 2006 GDP estimate down to 5.8 percent from 7.3 percent. [In 2007], the posted estimate is back up to 7.3, but we'll see how that number holds up after another summer season of high oil prices and drought—it may well prove to be overly optimistic once again.

Most global warming models agree that increasingly frequent and prolonged droughts are in East Africa's near future, which means that the problems these countries have faced in recent years are only going to worsen. Regrettably, dirty, destabilizing oil will be the quick fix unless alternatives are developed now.

The World Bank estimates that poverty has increased as much as 6 percent in some parts of the world due to the hike in oil prices in recent years. Especially vulnerable are the debt-burdened countries, particularly in Africa, which rely on oil imports to fuel their economy. The poorest countries in the world consume an almost negligible share of the millions of barrels of oil consumed every day globally, yet they are hit the most by rising world oil prices—and then hit again by the effects of climate change associated with burning hydrocarbons. This isn't a problem that can be solved by any single line of attack, but one thing is clear: until countries develop the tools to diversify their energy supplies away from conventional fossil fuels, the destabilizing effect of high oil prices will continue to undermine development efforts.

The Growing Opportunities

Rather than treating the symptoms of poverty, as development assistance too often does, investing in a clean energy future for poor countries gets at the roots of the development challenge. Renewable energy solutions can promote long-term economic growth and a built-in capacity for self-reliance.

The opportunities for Africa to emerge as a rising star in the growing renewable energy markets are enormous. A larger land mass than China, India, Western Europe, and the United States together, with thousands of miles of coastline and only 14 percent of the global population, Africa has vast, latent potential for wind and solar power generation. Recent studies show strong potential for wind power generation, not only in coastal South Africa, Morocco, and Madagascar, but also in Kenya and Ethiopia. In-depth evaluations are still pending for countries such as Namibia and Angola, where offshore wind currents are expected to be highly suitable for wind farming.

Or consider Kenya, which has already begun positioning itself to become a regional leader in photovoltaic [PV] cell assembly. With the introduction of lower-cost PV cells from China, the market price is due to drop dramatically over the coming decade, making wide-scale PV application much more feasible.

Along the Rift Valley fault that runs north to south through East Africa, geothermal activity could produce an estimated 9,000 megawatts of electricity using technology that could be deployed today—that's more than is currently produced globally—and could dramatically change the lives of hundreds of thousands of people in Ethiopia, Kenya, Uganda, Djibouti, Eritrea, and other African countries with substantial geothermal assets.

Biofuel is another sector where the continent could rival major global producers and play a central role in meeting the soaring demand for ethanol in Europe, United States, and China. Africa's arable lands are well-suited to a range of energy crops, especially in the tropical climate zones around the equator that enjoy optimal rains and a long growing season. Conventional feedstock crops like sugarcane, maize, and soy, as well as new oilseed crops, are already being grown and converted into biofuels.

Jatropha, for example, has attracted a fair amount of attention in recent years. A hardy bush thought to be appropriate for cultivation in Africa, Jatropha thrives in arid areas and can be grown on desert and marginal lands without taking land out of cultivation for food production and without requiring expensive inputs like fertilizers and water. Additionally, biofuel production would have cascading societal and economic advantages because as much as 60 percent of Africa's population makes a living from agriculture. Farmers who have seen their incomes steadily depreciate over the years following the slumping prices of agricultural commodities like coffee would find an appealing alternative in energy crops; with the refining process occurring domestically, a biofuel industry could create a high-value energy product for export.

With renewable energy markets growing annually by tens of billions of dollars, it's not surprisingly that African governments are anxious to capitalize on these opportunities. South Africa, for example, has been a leader in attracting investment in renewable energy, having recently unveiled an aggressive $800 million plan to launch a domestic biofuels industry.

Without due international focus and financing to back it up, transitioning into clean energy future will ... be a pipe dream for Africa.

But advances in clean energy go beyond the southern economic powerhouse. The president of Senegal, Abdoulaye Wade, has been one of the more proactive leaders on this front, and he's found a role model in ethanol-giant Brazil. A [2007] agreement between the two countries has the grand aspiration of spreading a Brazilian biofuels revolution to Africa through a series of technical and education exchanges.

The Senegalese president has also pioneered a so-called green OPEC [Organization of Petroleum Exporting Countries], which convenes a group of 13 non-petroleum-producing African nations with a mission to create jobs and enhance political and economic security by diversifying away from oil into clean energy. According to the United Nations, these countries collectively have hundreds of millions of hectares of arable land currently not being used that could be put into production for ethanol and biodiesel. Zambia, for its part, recently put hundreds of thousands of hectares under cultivation for biodiesel.

There are discrete rumblings of clean energy developments such as these across the continent, but more is needed and the need is urgent. Without due international focus and financing to back it up, transitioning into clean energy future will still be a pipe dream for Africa long after it's become a reality for the rest of the world. Particularly now, as African governments struggle to expand their energy infrastructures and build up the foundations for business and industrial manufacturing, we are presented with a critical window of opportunity.

A Population Explosion Threatens to Overwhelm Africa

Xan Rice

Xan Rice is the East Africa correspondent for the Guardian, *a British newspaper.*

There are 27.7 million people in Uganda. But by 2025 the population will almost double to 56 million, close to that of Britain, which has a similar land mass. In 44 years its population will have grown by nearly as much as China's.

"You look at these numbers and think 'that's impossible;" said Carl Haub, senior demographer at the US-based Population Reference Bureau, whose latest global projections show Uganda as the fastest growing country in the world. Midway through the 21st century Uganda will be the world's 12th most populous country with 130 million people—more than Russia or Japan.

By 2050 Chad, Mali, Guinea Bissau, Liberia, Niger, Burundi and Malawi—all among the poorest nations in the world—are projected to triple in size.

Startling as they are, the projections are feasible, and a glance at some of the variables shows why. A typical Ugandan woman gives birth to seven children—an extraordinarily high fertility rate that has remained largely unchanged for more than 30 years. Half the population is under 15, and will soon move into childbearing age. Fewer than one in five married women has access to contraception. Taken together, the factors point to a population explosion that has demographers and family planning experts warning that efforts to cut poverty are doomed unless urgent measures are taken.

And not just in Uganda. Across much of sub-Saharan Africa the population is expanding so quickly that the demographic map of the earth is changing. In the rest of world, including developing nations in Asia and South America, fertility rates have steadily declined to an average of 2.3 children to each mother. Most will experience only modest population growth in coming decades. Some countries, particularly in eastern Europe, will see their numbers decline.

But by 2050 Chad, Mali, Guinea Bissau, Liberia, Niger, Burundi and Malawi—all among the poorest nations in the world—are projected to triple in size. Nigeria will have become the world's fourth biggest country. Democratic Republic of Congo and Ethiopia will have vaulted into the top 10 for the first time. Nearly a quarter of the world's population will come from Africa—up from one in seven today.

"What's happening is alarming and depressing," said Jotham Musinguzi, director of the population secretariat in Uganda's ministry of finance, pointing out the clear correlation between high fertility levels and poverty. "Are we really going to be able to give these extra people jobs, homes, healthcare and education?"

Development may not be the only casualty of the population boom. With increased competition for scarce resources such as land, conflict is likely to increase. Consequences will be felt far beyond Africa: pressure to migrate abroad—already great—can only grow, experts say.

Cutting Fertility Rates

It is not yet a lost cause. Experience has shown that with strong political will population growth can be tackled in Africa. Southern Africa's population is expected to remain stable thanks to sustained efforts to cut fertility rates, although AIDS-related deaths are also a factor. In 1978 Uganda's neighbour Kenya had the world's highest fertility rate—more than eight children per mother. The government made family planning a national priority and by the mid-1990s the figure was less than five.

But a number of African leaders, including Uganda's president, Yoweri Museveni, believe that their countries are underpopulated, and that a bigger internal market and workforce will boost their economic prospects. In a speech . . . in July [2006], Mr Museveni said: "I am not one of those worried about the 'population explosion'. This is a great resource."

Studies across Africa have shown that the desire for large families remains powerful. In Nigeria a recent survey revealed that just 4% of women with two children said they wanted no more. Part of the reason is cultural, with bigger families seen as a sign of security. It is also because of fears of high levels of infant mortality.

Stigmas about birth control are another factor. Reproductive health experts say that a lack of information and of availability of female contraceptives plays a major role. In Ethiopia just 8% of married women use contraceptives. In Uganda more than a third of all women say they would like to stop—or at least stall—having children.

For that, donors must share in the blame, said Steven Sinding, director-general of the International Planned Parenthood Federation. He said the world had declared premature victory in the battle to cut fertility rates. Curbing population growth is not one of the UN's Millennium Development Goals, which aim to halve poverty by 2015, and barely features in the Commission for Africa report championed by [then British prime minister] Tony Blair.

"In Sub-Saharan Africa population remains a very serious problem," said Mr Sinding. "Yet donors have completely shifted their focus to HIV/AIDS and nobody is talking about it any more. Population is off the development agenda and that's a tragedy for Africa."

Elly Mugumya, head of the Family Planning Association of Uganda, agreed. In a tiny clinic in Kampala's Owino market, one of the biggest food and clothing bazaars in east Africa, he watched as six women—and two men—crammed into a tiny clinic to receive information about contraception. Cost is not the problem in Uganda, he explained: a three-month supply of birth-control pills costs 15p [pence]; condoms are free for the men. It is access—in most parts of Uganda clinics like this simply do not exist.

Global Warming Could Devastate Africa

Andrew Grice

Andrew Grice is the political editor of The Independent, *a British newspaper.*

Climate change could have a devastating impact on Africa, wiping out all the benefits from the measures to help the continent agreed by the world's richest nations [in 2005]. The warning . . . [was] issued by the British Government . . . [in 2006] when it announce[d] plans to bring poor countries into the next round of international discussions to combat global warming.

The serious threat posed to the developing world will be highlighted when Hilary Benn, the [British] Secretary of State for International Development, publishes his first White Paper setting out his department's strategy. It will warn that people in poor nations, while producing much lower carbon emissions than rich countries, could be the biggest victims of climate change.

They will have to cope with more droughts, more extreme temperatures and sudden and intense rainfall causing greater food insecurity, loss of income, higher death rates and more diseases. Research by the department to assess the impact on Africa by 2050, taking account of poverty forecasts, suggests that southern Africa and the Sahel, the Great Lakes areas, and the coastal zones of eastern and western Africa will be particularly at risk.

In some parts of east Africa, higher rainfall and and temperatures will help crop production in the short term but

Andrew Grice, "Global Warming 'Will Cancel Out Western Aid and Devastate Africa,'" *The Independent*, July 14, 2006. Reproduced by permission. www.independent.co.uk/environment/global-warming-will-cancel-out-western-aid-and-devastate-africa-407720.html.

there will be more frequent crop failures in the future. "What is clear is that Africa appears to have some of the greatest burdens of climate change impacts, certainly from the human health and agricultural perspective," the research concluded.

"It is a region with a generally limited ability to cope and adapt; and it has some of the lowest per capita emissions of the greenhouse gases that contribute to global warming. The likely impacts of climate change therefore present a global ethical challenge as well as a development and scientific challenge."

Finding Solutions

Mr. Benn will pledge that British ministers and officials will help developing nations address climate change. He will signal a shift under which, instead of relying on help from rich nations on dealing with the consequences, governments from poor countries play a key role in formulating the world's response to the issue. That would mean developing countries joining talks on a new international agreement on the threat to the planet, called "Kyoto 2".

[In] Africa, where the existence of widespread poverty, hunger and poor health already affect millions of people . . . climate change will make their lives even worse.

Mr. Benn does not want the world to impose carbon emissions targets on poor countries, which they would be reluctant to accept, but wants them to form part of a new global consensus on the issue. In the long run, that could allow them to "sell" carbon emissions permits to raise money for their own development.

Mr. Benn said: "Climate change is happening faster than any of us anticipated even five years ago. It is the most pressing global challenge of all, yet does not have a global framework for solving it. Climate change knows no boundaries and neither should we."

Gordon Conway, the chief scientific adviser at the [British] Department for International Development, said: "It is a phenomenon that occurs in a world that is already severely challenged. This is especially true of Africa, where the existence of widespread poverty, hunger and poor health already affect millions of people. All prognostications suggest climate change will make their lives even worse."

Tony Blair said he hoped Africa and climate change would be discussed by G8 [the eight most wealthy industrialized nations] leaders at their [2006] summit.... Jacques Chirac, the [then] French President, criticised the US for blocking progress on climate change. He said: "Global threats require global responses. We shall not solve the problem of global warming if we each go our own way or increase the number of unilateral or partial solutions. This is particularly true for global warming. I am concerned at the weakening of the international regime for climate change. We must reverse this trend."

President Chirac said the seven G8 members party to the Kyoto protocol snubbed by America, should set an example by respecting their commitments, as Europe and France were doing. "It is up to them to show the way forward for the post-2012 period," he said. "We seek an ambitious agreement commensurate with the threat posed to humanity, one committing all the G8 countries, including the United States, as well as emerging countries."

CHAPTER 2

Will International Aid Help Africa?

Chapter Preface

The U.S. foreign aid to Africa increasingly is coming not from the government but from the private sector. As the *Washington Times* reported in 2008, private aid to Africa now makes up 83 percent of the total U.S. aid to the continent. Fifty years ago, this situation was reversed, and government was the major provider of U.S. aid to the developing world. In the 1960s, for example, the U.S. government distributed about $5 billion annually to developing countries, while private sources contibuted only about $1.4 billion each year. By contrast, in 2005, the U.S. government disbursed about $27.6 billion in aid, roughly the same amount in real dollars as in the 1960s, while private aid for 2005 was about five times that amount, or around $136 billion.

Some of this private aid comes from churches and traditional charitable aid groups. Frequently, however, it also comes from very wealthy individual philanthropists and companies who want to help the developing world. One of the richest private philanthropic institutions, for example, is the Bill & Melinda Gates Foundation, a charitable organization created and endowed by the founder of Microsoft, the world's leading computer software company. Originally funded with $5 billion in 1999, the foundation has since poured billions of dollars into various health efforts, many of them focused on improving health care in Africa. Between 2000 and 2005, for example, the Gates Foundation donated a total of $900 million to two causes aimed at wiping out major diseases in Africa—the Global Fund to Fight AIDS, Tuberculosis and Malaria, and the Global Alliance for Vaccines and Immunizations, a coalition of international public health agencies, philanthropists, and drug companies created to develop and deliver vaccines for various diseases, including HIV, tuberculosis, and malaria. In 2006, the Gates Foundation turned its attention to Africa's agriculture industry, joining another charity, the Rockefeller Foundation, in a $150 million effort to create an Alliance for a Green Revolution in Africa (AGRA). Later, Gates added another $306 million to the cause. That same year, the Gates' endowment suddenly mushroomed when one of the world's richest men, Warren Buffett, gave most of his $40 billion fortune to the foundation. With this new infusion of cash, the Gates Foundation is expected to contribute as much as $2 billion per year to charitable causes.

Another new celebrity philanthropist concerned with helping Africa is Paul David Hewson, more commonly known as Bono, the lead singer in the Irish rock band U2. In 2002, Bono set up an organization called DATA (Debt, AIDS, Trade, Africa) to raise awareness about AIDS and other problems facing the continent. Bono also has pressured governments in the developed world to forgive debts and increase their foreign aid to all developing countries. In 2006, Bono helped to launch the ONE Campaign, an effort to convince U.S. officials to allocate an additional one percent of the U.S. budget toward providing basic needs for developing countries. The campaign calls for debt cancellation, trade reform, and anticorruption measures to be directed toward Africa and the world's poorest nations to help them conquer AIDS and extreme poverty. Other famous figures have also sought to raise awareness and aid for Africa, among them former U.S. president Bill Clinton and talk-show personality Oprah Winfrey.

Some of these private advocacy efforts have already been successful. In 2005, for example, Bono's advocacy was credited with helping to persuade the world's richest countries to forgive $40 billion in debt owed by the poorest nations—a decision that gave many developing nations the ability to spend more of their precious resources on critical problems such as poverty and health. And whether influenced by Bono or not, U.S. President George W. Bush over his two terms in office has tripled U.S. aid to Africa, from about $1.4 billion in 2001 to more than $4 billion annually. In addition, Bush recently pledged to increase U.S. humanitarian and development aid to the continent to almost $9 billion by 2010.

Both government donors and the new private philanthropists want to see results and are hoping that their efforts will make fundamental changes in Africa. The ultimate goal is for even the poorest African nations to finally solve their problems of poverty and disease and one day become economically self-sustaining and independent. Many commentators, such as economist Jeffrey Sachs, would like to see more development aid given to Africa to enable these changes to come about even more rapidly. Other development experts, however, such as economist William Easterly, argue that the industrialized nations have been providing aid to Africa for the last fifty years, with no real improvements in levels of hunger, poverty, or other developmental markers. Easterly and other critics believe that foreign aid has actually hurt Africa by making it dependent on handouts and stifling economic development. The authors in this chapter debate this central question of whether international aid, from both governments and the private sector, is beneficial or harmful for Africa.

Well-Targeted Foreign Aid
Is Helping Africa

Jeffrey D. Sachs

Jeffrey D. Sachs is a leading economist, director of the Earth In-stitute at Columbia University, and director of the United Na-tions Millennium Project, an effort to end poverty in the devel-oping world.

In a very different era, President John Kennedy declared

to those peoples in the huts and villages across the globe struggling to break the bonds of mass misery, we pledge our best efforts to help them help themselves, for whatever pe-riod is required—not because the Communists may be do-ing it, not because we seek their votes, but because it is right. If a free society cannot help the many who are poor, it cannot save the few who are rich.

It is difficult to imagine President [George W.] Bush mak-ing a similar pledge today, but he is far from alone in Wash-ington. The idea that the US should commit its best efforts to help the world's poor is an idea shared by Bill Gates, Warren Buffett, and Jimmy Carter, but it has been almost nowhere to be found in our capital. American philanthropists and non-profit groups have stepped forward while our government has largely disappeared from the scene.

There are various reasons for this retreat. Most impor-tantly, our policymakers in both parties simply have not at-tached much importance to this "soft" stuff, although their "hard" stuff is surely not working and the lack of aid is con-tributing to a cascade of instability and security threats in im-

Jeffrey D. Sachs, "How Aid Can Work," *New York Review of Books*, December 21, 2006. Copyright © 2006 NYREC, Inc. Reprinted with permission from the *New York Review of Books*. www.nybooks.com/articles/19721.

poverished countries such as Somalia. We are spending $550 billion per year on the military, against just $4 billion for Africa. Our African aid, incredibly, is less than three days of Pentagon spending, a mere $13 per American per year, and the equivalent of just 3 cents per $100 of US national income! The neglect has been bipartisan. The [Bill] Clinton administration allowed aid to Africa to languish at less than $2 billion per year throughout the 1990s.

A second reason for the retreat is the widespread belief that aid is simply wasted, money down the rat hole. That has surely been true of some aid, such as the "reconstruction" funding for Iraq and the cold war–era payouts to thugs such as Mobutu Sese Seko of Zaire. But these notorious cases obscure the critical fact that development assistance based on proven technologies and directed at measurable and practical needs—increased food production, disease control, safe water and sanitation, schoolrooms and clinics, roads, power grids, Internet connectivity, and the like—has a distinguished record of success.

Success of Well-Targeted Aid

The successful record of well-targeted aid is grudgingly acknowledged even by a prominent academic critic of aid, Professor Bill Easterly. Buried in his "Bah, Humbug" attack on foreign aid, *The White Man's Burden*, Mr. Easterly allows on page 176 [of that book] that

> foreign aid likely contributed to some notable successes on a global scale, such as dramatic improvement in health and education indicators in poor countries. Life expectancy in the typical poor country has risen from forty-eight years to sixty-eight years over the past four decades. Forty years ago, 131 out of every 1,000 babies born in poor countries died before reaching their first birthday. Today, 36 out of every 1,000 babies die before their first birthday.

Two hundred pages later Mr. Easterly writes that we should

put the focus back where it belongs: get the poorest people in the world such obvious goods as the vaccines, the antibiotics, the food supplements, the improved seeds, the fertilizer, the roads, the boreholes, the water pipes, the textbooks, and the nurses. This is not making the poor dependent on handouts; it is giving the poorest people the health, nutrition, education, and other inputs that raise the payoff to their own efforts to better their lives.

These things could indeed be done, if American officials weren't so consistently neglectful of development issues and with many too cynical to learn about the constructive uses of development assistance. They would learn that just as American subsidies of fertilizers and high-yield seed varieties for India in the late 1960s helped create a "Green Revolution" that set that vast country on a path out of famine and on to long-term development, similar support for high-yield seeds, fertilizer, and small-scale water technologies for Africa could lift that continent out of its current hunger-disease-poverty trap. They would discover that the Gates and Rockefeller Foundations have put up $150 million in the new Alliance for a Green Revolution in Africa to support the development and uptake of high-yield seed varieties there, an effort that the US government should now join and help carry out throughout sub-Saharan Africa.

They would also discover that the American Red Cross has learned—and successfully demonstrated—how to mass-distribute antimalaria bed nets to impoverished rural populations in Africa, with such success and at such low cost that the prospect of protecting all of Africa's children from that mass killer is now actually within reach. Yet they'd also learn that the Red Cross lacks the requisite funding to provide bed nets to all who need them. They would learn that a significant number of other crippling and killing diseases, including African river blindness, schistosomiasis, trauchoma, lymphatic filariasis, hookworm, ascariasis, and trichuriasis, could be brought under control for well under $2 per American citizen per year, and perhaps just $1 per American citizen!

A small fraction of [the] money [spent on the Iraq War]
... could save millions of lives and set entire regions on
a path of economic growth.

They would note, moreover, that the number of HIV-infected Africans on donor-supported antiretroviral therapy has climbed from zero in 2000 to 800,000 at the end of 2005, and likely to well over one million today. They would learn that small amounts of funding to help countries send children to school have proved successful in a number of African countries, so much so that the continent-wide goal of universal attendance in primary education is utterly within reach if financial support is provided.

As chairman of the Commission on Macroeconomics and Health of the World Health Organization (2000–2001) and director of the UN Millennium Project (2002–2006), I have led efforts that have canvassed the world's leading practitioners in disease control, food production, infrastructure development, water and sanitation, Internet connectivity, and the like, to identify practical, proven, low-cost, and scalable strategies for the world's poorest people such as those mentioned above.

Such life-saving and poverty-reducing measures raise the productivity of the poor so that they can earn and invest their way out of extreme poverty, and these measures do so at an amazingly low cost. To extend these proven technologies throughout the poorest parts of Africa would require around $75 billion per year from all donors, of which the US share would be around $30 billion per year, or roughly 25 cents per every $100 of US national income.

When we overlook the success that is possible, we become our own worst enemies. We stand by as millions die each year because they are too poor to stay alive. The inattention and neglect of our policy leaders lull us to believe casually that nothing more can be done. Meanwhile we spend hundreds of billions of dollars per year on military interventions doomed to fail, overlooking the fact that a small fraction of that money, if it were directed at development approaches, could save millions of lives and set entire regions on a path of economic growth. It is no wonder that global attitudes toward America have reached the lowest ebb in history. It is time for a new approach.

Only Foreign Aid Can Address Africa's Immediate Problems

Liz Dolan

Liz Dolan is one of the hosts of the nationally syndicated radio show Satellite Sisters. *She was formerly vice president of global marketing for sportswear giant Nike, Inc.*

Is foreign aid doing Africa more harm than good? That question surfaced very quickly in the opening session of TEDGlobal [a conference that seeks to generate ideas to solve world problems] in Arusha, Tanzania, sparking a lively point-counterpoint between Ugandan journalist Andrew Mwenda and unannounced guest Bono [of the band U2]. The conference, never before held in Africa, attracts a famously eclectic group, largely from the worlds of Technology, Entertainment and Design (hence the intials TED). In the room yesterday? Everyone from Google's Sergey Brin and [venture capital firm] Kleiner Perkins' John Doerr to primatolgist Jane Goodall and Ethiopian economist Eleni Gabre-Madhin, who is working on establishing the first Ethiopian Commodity Exchange.

I have made several trips to Africa before, most recently visiting Zambia with a group called Friends Of Zambia dedicated to attracting more foreign aid and trade to that small southern Africa country. I was so moved by what I saw in my stops at schools, orphanages and hospitals that I vowed to both stay involved personally and try to do what I could to bring the issue to the listeners of the talk radio show I host with my four sisters, *Satellite Sisters* on ABC Radio and XM. There are moments when the challenges seem so complex that you don't know where to begin, then you see that a village

Liz Dolan, "Is Foreign Aid Doing Africa More Harm than Good? Don't Try Telling Bono That," *The Huffington Post*, June 5, 2007. Copyright © 2007 HuffingtonPost.com, Inc. Reproduced by permission. www.huffingtonpost.com/liz-dolan/is-foreign-aid-doing-afri_b_50845.html.

just needs a well to get clean water or a girl just needs a uniform to go to school and you know where you can start.

The Debate on Aid to Africa

One of the opening speakers at TEDGlobal was Andrew Mwenda, a Uganda journalist and fellow at Stanford. He voiced a point of view that I have been hearing more of lately: that the foreign aid provided by developed nations is doing more harm than good by propping up corrupt governments and turning the citizens into passive recipients of charity instead of active parts in the building of their countrys' economy. It's direct foreign investment that will begin to change the economic dynamic here, not charity.

Based on the reaction from audience members from 40 different countries with a large African concentration, Mwenda's position was widely held. To make his point, Mwenda took a few swipes at the Marshall Plan that rebuilt Europe after the Second World War, claiming "it was not as great as it was cracked up to be." Then he challenged the audience to "give me a single example of one country that was developed with aid. Just give me one example."

You have to work on the micro as well as the macro economic issues.

That's when some gentle heckling began from a familiar Irish voice in the audience. Most people in the hall did not even realize Bono was there. After a short break he took the stage with a short video from German Chancellor and G8 [the group of the eight most industrialized nations] chair Angela Merkel and this opening line: "Try telling Angela Merkel that the Marshall Plan was a load of crap." Bono, one of the world's most visible proponents of debt relief and massive development aid to Africa from the G8, said Germany was a "brilliant example" of how aid can work. "It was a bulwark against sovietism [communism] and also an act of mercy." He went on to say that "the Cold War was fought in Africa, too. We were complicit in supporting murderous regimes like Mobutu's. I don't think it is charity to pay back those countries several generations later. It is justice."

Addressing the growing feeling that debt relief will not get African nations nearly as far as western direct investment, Bono said "You'd think somebody farted in here when the words 'debt relief' came up—ooh, debt relief, that's so uncool. Well, I will tell you that 20 million children in Africa are going to school today as a direct result of debt relief, 3 million right here in Tanzania alone. The reason Ireland now has one of the hottest economies in the world and gets all this direct investment from companies like Google and Intel is that they realized Ireland had an extremely well-educated population. Even I was extremely well-educated," he joked. "Combine a well-educated population with the kinds of tax relief that was offered to companies coming in and you have economic growth. Only the state can offer that package."

I don't know exactly what every individual should do but I do believe that no one should be doing nothing.

To Mwenda's charge that every minister in every bloated department has a fleet of cars, yet few dispensaries have even a single ambulance, Bono conceded that "this can't be about redecorating presidential palaces" but reminded the audience that "3000 African kids will die today of malaria so you have to work on the micro as well as the macro economic issues." . . .

Doing Something

It's too simple to decide that either aid or trade is the solution, though I was surprised to hear from journalist Carol Pineau, the producer of the documentary *Africa: Open for Business* that "no one in Africa really believes any more that aid does any good at all." Really? That shocks me. I believe ultimately that it is jobs and business and sustainable industries that will be the most powerful tools for lifting up these countries, but can free market forces save the people dying of AIDS right now? I don't see how. I have worried in the past that because so many of the resources that come to Africa come in the form of aid, that Africa's best and brightest are working for NGO's [nongovernmental organizations] and charities, instead of starting their own small businesses. [In 2005] I met a fantastic young man in Lusaka, Zambia, running an orphanage. His managerial skills were so impressive that I couldn't help thinking to myself whether the country would be better served if this young man were given the money to start a business instead of an orphanage. Does aid create a brain drain away from agriculture and industry and towards relief work? It clearly can.

But for me, as one American woman with a radio audience of many American women, I've got to think that I belong in the camp that's helping to respond to the day-to-day needs on the ground of girls and women who are just trying to make a life for themselves and their communities. I don't know exactly what every individual should do but I do believe that no one should be doing nothing.

Increasing Aid and Improving Distribution Methods Will Help Africa

United Nations Conference on Trade and Development

The United Nations Conference on Trade and Development (UNCTAD) promotes the integration of developing countries into the world economy.

Aid to Africa not only should be doubled, as now agreed to by donors, but most of it should be distributed multilaterally, perhaps by a UN fund independent of political pressures, a new UNCTAD report contends.

The money should be released in predictable tranches [portions] over a long-term period, should be more focused than currently on enabling African economies to produce a broader range of goods and to create more jobs, and should be channelled to those countries' general budgets so that their legislatures can best decide how to spend it, the report recommends.

Such an arrangement would replace the current chaotic system in which too many agencies—some bilateral, some multilateral—are pushing too many development projects that sometimes compete with each other, often don't match recipients' development goals, are costly to administer, and frequently leave African governments confused and stymied by their numerous rules and conditions, says *Economic Development in Africa 2006: Doubling Aid: Making the "Big Push" Work.*

Back to the Future

The report says a new "aid architecture" is needed, drawing in part on the Marshall Plan that helped revitalize European economies after World War II. That plan, paid for by the United States, recognized that shock therapy and piecemeal projects had not helped in getting Western Europe back on its feet and offered instead a generous, multi-year and coordinated funding approach, with each State drawing up long-term recovery plans with no outside interference. The US released aid in predictable tranches predominantly through grants, and while intermediate targets were used to measure progress, rules and conditions on the aid were applied in a flexible manner. Such principles were largely forgotten as international aid programmes expanded in the 1980s, the report says, although the European Union's [EU] own regional funds have functioned well under a similar approach. These funds also have a clear focus on strengthening investment, multi-year funding, strong local ownership, and clearly stated aims to strengthen State capacities.

Existing multilateral aid mechanisms, such as the World Bank's International Development Association . . . , have not lived up to expectations.

Given the basic challenges across the region, much of this initial push will be frontloaded on the public sector where the preferred modality of support from the international community should be in the form of grants to the national budget. These should come with limited conditionality and should help strengthen public sector management. Donors should abide by their commitments to significantly raise the share of direct budget support, currently just 20% of bilateral flows to sub-Saharan Africa (SSA).

Going Multilateral

In recent years, the international community has begun to turn its attention to the quality of aid. But the report worries that the right balance is still not being struck. It notes that while aid flows have on average risen sharply since their low point in the late 1990s, much of this rise has been accounted for by debt relief and with a handful of what some critics call "aid darlings" receiving much of the increased flow. Moreover, the change in emphasis has not stopped a repoliticization of aid flows: since the early 1990s, the focus of EU aid has shifted to Eastern Europe and Mediterranean countries; security issues have recently become a principal concern for some donors; and opening markets weigh as heavily as ever on deciding who gets what.

With this in mind, the report suggests that the time is "perhaps right to revisit the idea, first broached in the 1950s, of a UN funding window" tailored to African development needs. Such an approach "can help to reduce unnecessary and costly competition among donors, and thus greatly reduce administration costs. It can also provide a buttress against the politicization of aid which has been so damaging in the past."

The report states that existing multilateral aid mechanisms, such as the World Bank's International Development Association (IDA) and the International Monetary Fund's Poverty Reduction and Growth Facility, have not lived up to expectations and are not suited to administering doubled aid. Net disbursements by IDA to SSA, for example, are under US$3 billion, around 10% of all flows, and depend on difficult replenishment exercises. These funds along with various new mechanisms related to a doubling of aid might best be merged into a new UN fund, the report suggests. Such a Fund could act as a magnet for new proposals such as the International Finance Facility suggested by the United Kingdom's Chancellor of the Exchequer. The report also sees the need for a multilateral forum within the UN, similar to that already established at the Organization for Economic Cooperation and Development [OECD—an organization that helps governments with the challenges of a globalized economy], to give an airing to the concerns of recipients as aid increases.

Other shortcomings of current aid systems for Africa, the report contends, are that they are focused on short-term results, have too high a technical assistance component and are increasingly targeted at social sectors, which, while important, don't address the needs of African countries to build the productive infrastructure and capacities that will enable them to diversify and upgrade their economies. These changes require long-term attention but have the advantage of offering a way out of the poverty cycle and—for donor nations—a potential end to ever-increasing requests for aid.

Increased aid can give a "big push" to [Africa], sparking a virtuous circle of higher rates of savings, investment and economic growth as a route to a permanent reduction in poverty.

To meet the Millennium Development Goals [to eliminate poverty], it is estimated that African economies must grow at roughly 8% per year. Without more attention to their productive capacities, the report says, most will fall well short of the mark, yet in sub-Saharan Africa, the share of social sectors in total technical cooperation rose from 50% in the early 1990s to 70% [in 2006], with corresponding falls in the share taken by infrastructure, productive sectors and agriculture.

A Failed Aid-Adjustment Nexus

Africa has received some $500 billion in aid since 1980, around $30 per capita annually, the report notes. Since real incomes fell over this period in many countries, sceptics have raised questions about whether further increases in aid really offer a route out of poverty. In fact, the major trend between the early 1980s and the late 1990s was declining real per-capita aid flows to SSA which were wholly insufficient to offset the resources lost to declining commodity prices leading to mounting indebtedness; let alone recurrent famines and the HIV crisis; and it was often volatile in nature. Moreover, it was conditioned on recipients adopting a standardized package of adjustment measures including price stabilization, rapid liberalization, and privatization that imposed austerity in many countries.

UNCTAD's examination of successful experiences—for example, East Asia in the 1950s and '60s and Ireland from the early 1970s, enjoyed much larger aid flows than have most African countries—indicates that increased aid can give a "big push" to the region, sparking a virtuous circle of higher rates of savings, investment and economic growth as a route to a permanent reduction in poverty. However, the delivery of aid and accompanying policies have to be re-thought, taking into account such factors as Africa's vulnerability to external shocks, its binding structural constraints on growth prospects, and the inefficiency of the current aid system.

The report also contends that a careful weighing of the evidence shows that many of the concerns raised by sceptics, such as the insufficient absorptive capacity of African economies or the distortion of price incentives—such as the "Dutch disease"—are exaggerated and can be managed.

Aid Patterned on the Marshall Plan Will Help Africa

Glenn Hubbard and William Duggan

Glenn Hubbard is dean of the Columbia University School of Business and served as chairman of the Council of Economic Advisers under President George W. Bush from 2001 to 2003. William Duggan is an associate professor at the Columbia University School of Business and a former Ford Foundation representative for West Africa.

Sixty years ago [in 1947], George Marshall, US secretary of state, announced what became known as the Marshall plan for Europe in an address at Harvard University. The Marshall plan has been widely heralded as an example of the triumph of foreign aid on a grand scale. Given the high rate of extreme poverty in sub-Saharan Africa, and that Africa is poorer today than 20 years ago, some leaders have called for a Marshall plan for Africa.

We agree.

A real Marshall plan for Africa would stand apart from the aid system of governments and non-governmental organisations.

An African Marshall Plan

But the original Marshall plan was less a grand aid programme than a targeted effort to restore the power of business as a growth engine. A true Marshall plan for Africa could ignite growth and reduce poverty, but only through a different set of institutions than the current aid system.

The plan had four main elements. First, a rich country—the US—made grants to European governments for restoring production through loans to local businesses which repaid them to their own governments. Second, each European government spent the repaid funds on restoring commercial infrastructure to boost production, such as ports and railways. Third, each European government made economic policy reforms to support their domestic private sectors. Fourth, a regional co-ordinating body handled the distribution of funds among countries.

Grand foreign aid plans have little in common with the original Marshall plan. Aid plans foster government-led development with an emphasis on social services. The Marshall plan fostered business-sector development with an emphasis on loans and economic infrastructure. It was something that Africa has never seen on a large scale—a business-sector support project.

A real Marshall plan for Africa would stand apart from the aid system of governments and non-governmental organisations [NGOs]. The original Marshall plan had its own institutions: it created an Economic Co-operation Administration [ECA] to run the entire programme, with headquarters in Washington and small missions in every European country. Each country had a special ECA account. Receiving countries formed a regional co-ordinating body, the Organisation for European Economic Co-operation, which led to both the OECD [Organisation for Economic Cooperation and Development] and the European Union.

An African Marshall plan would have its own institutions along international, regional and national lines. The equivalent of an ECA would collect and manage donor funds. A country would become eligible through specific policies in place to foster business development. In the original Marshall plan, governments spent the repaid loans on economic infrastructure projects the ECA approved. An African plan could do the same. Given Africa's size, there might be regional ECAs rather than a single one. The Marshall plan was competitive among countries: if one did not co-operate, another country was happy to take the funds instead. An African Marshall plan would do the same.

Business Sector Is Key

This leads to the second key element of a real African Marshall plan: the business sector must lead it. Business leaders staffed the original Marshall plan, including its head, Paul Hoffman of carmaker Studebaker.

An African Marshall plan would do only business development. Africa has tremendous social needs that call for concentrated attention from expert agencies: that is the proper role for governments and NGOs. Yet those same aid agencies contain many small units that have pioneered support for African business. An African Marshall plan would expand the best practice of those agencies from a sideshow to the main event in African aid. For example, there are already programmes to improve African business schools, which can provide the same support for the business sector as in rich countries around the world.

Marshall's logic applies to Africa today: a thriving business sector is the key to improving political and social progress.

With a business core, it is likely that it would be less popular than grand aid schemes—after all, charity touches the heart and business does not. The original Marshall plan started out with only 14 per cent of the US public in support. The tide for action was turned by an aggressive information campaign by US business leaders, in this case the Committee for

Economic Development. By contrast, business leaders have been conspicuously absent from the growing debate on African poverty.

In his speech, Marshall was very clear that the "breakdown of the business structure of Europe during the war" was the problem aid must solve. "Our . . . purpose should be the revival of a working economy in the world so as to permit the emergence of political and social conditions in which free institutions can exist. Such assistance, I am convinced, must not be on a piecemeal basis as various crises develop."

Marshall's logic applies to Africa today: a thriving business sector is the key to improving political and social progress. Aid must help, not hinder, and reform itself. Otherwise, Africa is doomed.

Paternalistic Aid Programs Keep Africa Enslaved

Michael Knox Beran

Michael Knox Beran is a lawyer and author, as well as a contributing editor for City Journal, *an urban-policy magazine published in New York City.*

Paternalism was supposed to be finished. The belief that grown men and women are childlike creatures who can thrive in the world only if they submit to the guardianship of benevolent mandarins underlay more than a century's worth of welfare-state social policy beginning with Otto von Bismarck's first *Wohlfahrtsstaat* experiments in nineteenth-century Germany. But paternalism's centrally directed systems of subsidies failed to raise up submerged classes, and by the end of the twentieth century even many liberals, surveying the cultural wreckage left behind by the Great Society, had abandoned their faith in the welfare state.

Yet in one area, foreign aid, the paternalist spirit is far from dead. A new generation of economists and activists is calling for a "big push" in Africa to expand programs that in practice institutionalize poverty rather than end it. The Africrats' enthusiasm for the failed policies of the past threatens to turn a struggling continent into a permanent ghetto—and to block the progress of ideas that really can liberate Africa's oppressed populations.

The New Paternalism

The intellectual cover for the new paternalism comes from economists like Columbia's Jeffrey Sachs, who in his recent bestseller *The End of Poverty* argues that prosperous nations can dramatically reduce African poverty, if not eliminate it, by increasing their foreign-aid spending and expanding smaller assistance programs into much larger social welfare regimes. "The basic truth," Sachs says, "is that for less than a percent of the income of the rich world"—0.7 percent of its GNP [gross national product] for the next 20 years—"nobody has to die of poverty on the planet."

Sachs headed the United Nations' Millennium Project, created in 2002 by UN Secretary-General Kofi Annan to figure out how to reverse poverty, hunger, and disease in poor countries. After three years of expensive lucubration [laborious study], the project's ten task forces concluded that prosperous nations can indeed defeat African poverty by 2025—if only they spend more money. "The world already has the technology and know-how to solve most of the problems faced in the poor countries," a Millennium report asserted. "As of 2006, however, these solutions have still not been implemented at the needed scale." Translation: the developed nations have been too stingy.

We've heard this before. The "response of the West to Africa's tragedy has been constant throughout the years," observes NYU [New York University] economist William Easterly. From [economic historian] Walt Rostow and [former U.S. president] John F. Kennedy in 1960 to Sachs and [former British prime minister] Tony Blair today, the message, Easterly says, has been the same: "Give more aid." Assistance to Africa, he notes, "did indeed rise steadily throughout this period (tripling as a percent of African GDP [gross domestic product] from the 1970s to the 1990s)," yet African growth "remained stuck at zero percent per capita."

All told, the West has given some $568 billion in foreign aid to Africa over the last four decades, with little to show for it. Between 1990 and 2001, the number of people in sub-Saharan Africa below what the UN calls the "extreme poverty line"—that is, living on less than $1 a day—increased from

227 million to 313 million, while their inflation-adjusted average daily income actually fell, from 62 cents to 60. At the same time, nearly half the continent's population—46 percent—languishes in what the UN defines as ordinary poverty.

Like earlier practitioners of paternalist charity, today's Africrats propose policies that treat the material effects of Africa's problems . . . not their underlying causes.

Yet notwithstanding this record of failure, the prosperous nations' heads of state have sanctioned Sachs's plan to throw more money at Africa's woes. In July 2005, G-8 leaders [from the top eight richest industrial nations] meeting in Gleneagles, Scotland, endorsed Sachs's Millennium thesis and promised to double their annual foreign aid from $25 billion to $50 billion, with at least half the money earmarked for Africa. This increased spending, the Gleneagles principals proclaimed, will "lift tens of millions of people out of poverty every year." No doubt, too, Africans will soon be extracting sunbeams from cucumbers.

Celebrity Africrats

It is doubtful whether the G-8 leaders themselves believe all the gaseous rhetoric that emanates from their meetings. But a sort of fifth estate, composed of actors and aging rock stars, has emerged, determined to hold the prodigal statesmen to their word. The new Africrats include pop empress Madonna, actress Angelina Jolie, and U2 singer Paul Hewson, better known as Bono, who has emerged as Sachs's leading promoter and enforcer. After attending this year's [2008] G-8 summit at Heiligendamm, Germany, Bono pronounced himself "skeptical" of the pledges made at Gleneagles. The skepticism was reasonable, given that the document in question was not intended to be credible. But Bono, who wrote the foreword to Sachs's *The End of Poverty*, has made it his life's work to force the G-8 to take its oratory seriously. At Heiligendamm, he got into what he called a "huge row" with the Germans, whom he accused of "playing a numbers game" with their aid contributions.

Bono has had better luck with U.S. leaders. In 2002, he and then–[US] treasury secretary Paul O'Neill traveled together to Africa on a widely publicized 12-day "fact-finding" mission to study the AIDS epidemic. This year [2008] President [George W.] Bush, who reportedly discussed increasing American aid to Africa with Bono at Heiligendamm, announced that he would expand the centerpiece of his Africa policy, the President's Emergency Plan for AIDS Relief. Bush launched the initiative in 2003 with a five-year, $15 billion commitment; in May [2007], he asked Congress to approve an additional $30 billion.

The Problem with Handouts

Like earlier practitioners of paternalist charity, today's Africrats propose policies that treat the material effects of Africa's problems—disease, dirty water, hunger—not their underlying causes, which the West, too, once struggled with. For thousands of years, high rates of death from infectious diseases were the norm throughout the world. Before the twentieth century, Western parents expected to lose at least one of their children to illnesses that are preventable today. Not until late in the nineteenth century did the White House itself have clean water; in 1862, Abraham Lincoln's son Willie died of typhoid, likely contracted from the mansion's tainted plumbing. Hunger, too, once darkened what is now the prosperous world, though so effectively has the problem been solved that countries like the United States face a looming obesity crisis.

How did today's prosperous nations create the embarrassment of riches that they now enjoy? No benign magician descended, *à la* Jeffrey Sachs, on London or Washington to shower its inhabitants with money. Instead, the rich nations developed laws and freedoms that enabled people to take their futures into their own hands. As Peruvian economist Hernando de Soto has argued in *The Mystery of Capital: Why Capitalism Triumphs in the West and Fails Everywhere Else*, the world's poorest countries remain poor in part because they lack legal protections—property rights foremost among them—that enable people in the West to tap the potential of "dead" capital and invest it in wealth-generating enterprises.

Not only do the Africrats' policies fail to address the real causes of Africa's troubles; they treat the people whom they are trying to help as children.

Kenyan economist James Shikwati agrees that handouts thwart the emergence of a culture of self-reliant problem solving and that they breed corruption to boot. When a drought afflicts Kenya, he says, Kenyan politicians "reflexively cry out for more help." Their calls reach the United Nations World Food Program, a "massive agency of apparatchiks [minor bureaucrats] who are in the absurd situation of, on the one hand, being dedicated to the fight against hunger while, on the other hand, being faced with unemployment were hunger actually eliminated." When the requested grain reaches Africa, a portion of it "often goes directly into the hands of unscrupulous politicians who then pass it on to their own tribe to boost their next election campaign." Much of the rest of the grain gets dumped at less than fair market value. "Local farmers may as well put down their hoes right away," Shikwati says. "No one can compete with the UN's World Food Program."

CARE, one of the world's largest charities, would agree. In August [2007], it rejected some $45 million in U.S. government financing to distribute subsidized food in Africa, saying that the subsidies hurt African farmers. "If someone wants to help you, they shouldn't do it by destroying the very thing that they're trying to promote," George Odo, a CARE official, told the *New York Times*. The American government, however, has no plans to scrap the practice. . . .

Treating Africans as Children

Not only do the Africrats' policies fail to address the real causes of Africa's troubles; they treat the people whom they are trying to help as children. *Vanity Fair's* [2007] Africa issue described how Sachs, in a southwestern Ugandan village addressed the inhabitants as though they were slightly dim kindergartners:

> "And we have seen the bed nets in your houses. Do you have bed nets in your houses?"
>
> "Yes!"
>
> "We are happy to see that. And are they working? Do they help?"
>
> "Yes!"
>
> "We are happy to see that." . . .

In 2004, Prince Harry of England visited Lesotho, a small, landlocked country in southern Africa, to befriend children with AIDS; in front of cameras, the prince gave a four-year-old boy a pair of Wellington boots and cradled a six-month-old girl in his arms. When Madonna traveled to Malawi in 2006, dripping dollars and sentiment, her publicist spoke candidly of her paternalist (or maternalist) aspirations: "She's kind of adopting an entire country of children."

If the prosperous nations really want to help Africa, . . . they need to promote . . . wealth-generating entrepreneurial effort.

Rotimi Sankore, a journalist who has written widely on Africa, points out that the Africrats' favorite poster child is "a skeletal looking two- or three-year-old brown-skinned girl in a dirty torn dress, too weak to chase off dozens of flies settling on her wasted and diseased body, her big round eyes pleading for help." Sankore calls such images "development pornography." The "subliminal message, unintended or not," he argues, "is that people in the developing world require indefinite and increasing amounts of help and that without aid charities and donor support, these poor incapable people in Africa or Asia will soon be extinct through disease and starvation."

Kenyan writer Binyavanga Wainaina maintains that the relentless focus of the Africrats on the image of the pitiable, childish African distorts Africans' idea of themselves and their potential. "There must be a change in mentality," agrees Kenya's Shikwati. "We have to stop perceiving ourselves as beggars." At the same time, Africrat rhetoric that depicts the continent as "one giant crisis" (Wainaina's phrase) obscures the progress that many Africans are making on their own. The African entrepreneurs who make up what Wainaina calls the "equity generation"—stock exchanges now thrive in Uganda, Kenya, Nigeria, and Ghana—are, by pursuing their own private interests, doing more to assure a prosperous African future than all the Africrats' programs put together. President Bush has made subsidized medicine the centerpiece of his Africa policy; he might do better to invest in Africa's rising entrepreneurs. . . .

If the prosperous nations really want to help Africa, they need to resist the seductions of paternalism. They need to promote, not policies that will ensure that the continent remains a collection of fiefdoms dependent on subsidies and celebrity pity, but wealth-generating entrepreneurial effort. They need to export, not a dated philosophy of mandarinism, but ideas that really can lift peoples and nations out of the lower depths.

Foreign Aid Is the Worst Plan for Helping Africa

Walter E. Williams

Walter E. Williams is a syndicated columnist and a professor of economics at George Mason University in Fairfax, Virginia.

President [George W.] Bush's [2008] trip to Africa and promise of increased foreign aid will do little or nothing to solve the ongoing tragedy in most places on the south-of-Sahara African continent. Kenya is on the brink of a civil war. Over 1,000 people have been killed and another 300,000 made homeless. Rebels have invaded Chad. In the Darfur region of the Sudan, millions of people have been displaced in a genocidal war. Ethiopia and Eritrea threaten war again. Somalian warlords are in a pitched battle. Zimbabwe, once an independent, thriving jewel on the continent, now ruled by a tyrant, is on the brink of disaster, experiencing a 66,000 percent rate of inflation, expected to be over 100,000 percent by [2008's] end. To put that inflation in perspective, the government has recently started printing 10 million Zimbabwe dollar notes. A hamburger sells for 15 million Zimbabwe dollars.

The recent African carnage is by no means new. During a 100-day period in 1994, an estimated 800,000 Rwandans, mostly Tutsis, were killed. There were an estimated 100,000 to 500,000 Ugandans murdered under the brutal rule of Idi Amin. Liberia, Ivory Coast and the Congo have been racked by war, and slavery exists to this day in Mauritania and Sudan. Added to this carnage is gross corruption, AIDS, famine and repression.

Walter E. Williams, "Worst Plan for Africa: Foreign Aid," *WorldNetDaily.com*, February 27, 2008. Copyright © 2008. Reproduced by permission. www.worldnetdaily.com/index.php?fa=PAGE.view&pageId=57412.

The Problem of African Dictators

African leaders, and many people on the left, blame Africa's problems on the evils of colonialism. They sometimes blame the violence on the borders colonialists created that ignored ethnicity. Many African nations have been independent for four decades. If colonial borders were a major problem, how come they haven't changed them? And, by the way, colonialism cannot explain Third World poverty. Some of today's richest countries are former colonies, such as: United States, Canada, Australia, New Zealand and Hong Kong. Some of today's poorest countries were never colonies, such as: Ethiopia, Liberia, Tibet, Nepal and Bhutan. The colonialism argument is simply a cover up for African dictators.

Most of what Africa needs the West cannot give: rule of law, private property rights, fewer economic restrictions, independent judiciary and limited government.

The worst thing the West can do to Africa is to give more foreign aid. For the most part, foreign aid is government to government. As such, it provides the financial resources that enable Africa's grossly corrupt and incompetent regimes to buy military equipment, pay off cronies and continue to oppress their people. It also provides resources for the leaders to live lavishly and set up "retirement" accounts in foreign banks.

An African Problem

Africa is the world's most natural-resources-rich continent. It has 50 percent of the world's gold, most of the world's diamonds and chromium, 90 percent of the cobalt, 40 percent of the world's potential hydroelectric power, 65 percent of the manganese, and millions of acres of untilled farmland, as well as other natural resources. Before independence, every African country was self-sufficient in food production; today, many depend on imports and others stand at the brink of famine.

The only people who can solve the problems of Africa are Africans themselves. It is only they who can change their leaders, end corruption and bring about transparency in government and end the African wars. Only they can stop the continent's massive brain drain. This was brought home to me, a number of years ago, at a dinner I was invited to in honor of a new Nigerian ambassador to the United States. During his speech, he admonished the Nigerian professionals in attendance to come home to help the country develop. The Nigerians seated at my table, and nearby tables, fell into quiet laughter.

Most of what Africa needs the West cannot give: rule of law, private property rights, fewer economic restrictions, independent judiciary and limited government. The one important thing we can do to help is to lower our trade barriers.

Africa Must Create Its Own Destiny

Ferial Haffajee

Ferial Haffajee is the editor of the Mail & Guardian, *a South African newspaper.*

Africa. South Africa. Nigeria. Darfur. Swaziland. Côte d'Ivoire. These are not places we can leave behind. We live there. [U2 lead singer] Bono's great, but he is your wake-up call, not ours. Africa is too big for sound bites—and too complex for generalizations.

Imagine that Europe should be thus covered: "The Hopeless Continent. Its economic heart (Germany) is broken, the mafia is threatening a fragile new government (Italy)—and London is being bombed as [then–British prime minister] Tony Blair refuses to let go of the reins of power."

"Strikers control the streets (France). Growth is anemic and Islamic fundamentalism is wreaking havoc from Amsterdam to Istanbul, where a judge was shot and killed by a terrorist last week."

"The Red Dragon's breathing fire, the Bollywood beast is catching up. Europe is a hopeless continent. How shall we save it?" This is nonsense, of course—as it is nonsense to speak of an African dilemma or an African solution. You know the story. But often I wonder if you know the whole story.

Peer Review

A few months ago, South Africa held a congress of the people. In Kliptown, hundreds of delegates from government and civil society met to give our country a national assessment. How do we do on governance? What is our democratic temperature? It was the system called peer review in practice. Ordinary people had an opportunity to say what they think of everything from judicial independence to their welfare payments.

When was the last time you had such a say outside of an election? Peer review is setting a precedent on our continent. Enshrined in the African Union, it ends the absolute sovereignty that allowed so many abuses to go unchecked in old Africa.

Our continent must be the architect of its own destiny.

Yes, the system of peer review can be swaddled in red tape. Yes, it is slow and the government has a big say. But this notion that we are our brothers' and sisters' keeper is new— and it is happening. There are African solutions beyond Bono.

The winds of change also blew through Nigeria . . . [in 2006], when senators told President Olusegun Obasanjo, in no uncertain terms, that he should not stay for a third term. If only [current British prime minister] Gordon Brown . . . had such luck [getting Tony Blair to hand over the reins of power].

Africa Beyond Aid

However, not everybody has felt the winds of change, of course, as the mad ramblings of Zimbabwe's Robert Mugabe and the mass arrests of opponents by Ethiopia's Meles Zenawi attest. I make no pretence that all is well in Africa. It is not. But, our continent must be the architect of its own destiny.

With Afghanistan exploding again, Iraq on the edge of a civil war—and Iran now in U.S. President George W. Bush's periscope, it is no surprise that Africa will once again fall off the radarscreen.

It is my view that we must begin to see an Africa beyond aid. The Brenthurst Foundation has calculated that post-colonial Africa has received $580 billion in donor funds—to no great effect.

Of course, war, corruption and instability will always militate against aid effectiveness, but with African well-being hardly inching up the development indices, is aid the answer? Increasingly we must realize that it is not the answer—or at least not all of the answer. There is no argument for immediate self-sufficiency. Not for the hungry people of Zimbabwe. Not for the displaced people of Darfur. Aid for humanitarian purposes is—and will be—necessary in Africa for the foreseeable future.

But securing stability and sustainable well-being must come through other means. What might those be? Fair trade and debt relief offer a far more sustainable path towards security and development. African economic growth is steady near the level of 5% a year, but it will take growth of 7% a year to meet the challenges of the Millennium Development Goals [the UN plan to eliminate poverty] for decent living standards.

This will require much better terms of trade. The oil rush is aiding investment, but not enough oil revenues are reaching the people. In agriculture, we stand a real chance. If the barriers to entry into wealthy markets are lowered, investment could increase and employment could grow.

If the media around the world makes sure that the continent ... is covered in all its complexity, we will have no need next year to decry another forgotten year.

In addition, our continent needs to harness its diaspora [Africans who have left Africa] as India has done. In a global age, there is no use decrying the fact that there are more

South African nurses in Dubai than there are in Soweto, more Ugandan doctors in San Francisco than in Uganda.

Changing Circumstances

Remittances should be leveraged. Every year, a whopping $100 billion is transferred by migrants to their home countries. In some areas, these remittances are paying a development dividend.

From a call center in Cape Town, where Africa can find a spot in the global growth in services, to Kenya's flower farms, the solutions are different. From Darfur's intractable peace talks to Congo's election in late July 2006, so are its problems.

If the media around the world makes sure that the continent maintains its place on the news agenda and that it is covered in all its complexity, we will have no need next year to decry another forgotten year.

CHAPTER 3

Will Trade Benefit African Nations?

Chapter Preface

Countries and companies have always traded with each other, but during the last few decades of the twentieth century, trading became much more of a global phenomenon. Global trade blossomed partly as a result of advancements in communications and other technologies and partly due to the promotion of liberal, or so-called free, global trade policies by developed countries such as the United States and Great Britain. Although this new global trading system has benefited many companies and brought new wealth to many industrialized nations, critics have charged that globalization policies have brought only increased poverty and greater economic underdevelopment to many developing countries.

The main concern of critics is what they view as unfair global trade rules. Under global trade policies promoted by the United States and international trade organizations such as the World Trade Organization (WTO) and the International Monetary Fund (IMF), many developing countries have been encouraged to eliminate protections for their products and tariffs on imported goods, and to open their economies to foreign investment and global trade. Meanwhile, highly developed countries such as the United States and Great Britain continued to maintain subsidies and trade barriers to protect some of their industries from global competition. One of the most glaring inequities in the global trade system, critics say, involves developing countries' refusal to abandon government protections for their agricultural products. Many developing countries in Africa have rural, farm-based economies and would greatly benefit by selling their agricultural products to the developing world. But the rich countries' farm subsidies and trade tariffs block African agricultural commerce from these lucrative foreign markets. Many commentators also criticize developing countries for giving their excess food as aid to

Africa, because this further undermines African farmers by reducing the local demand for their agricultural products.

These and other criticisms of global free trade led to a new series of multinational trade talks launched at Doha, Qatar, in 2001, designed to promote fairer trade with developing countries. The goals of the Doha trade negotiations included correcting the inequities of previous trade agreements, giving developing nations more flexibility in developing their economies, and eliminating agricultural subsidies in the developed countries.

The Doha talks, however, have so far failed to reach these goals. The talks collapsed at a 2003 summit in Cancún, Mexico, when developing countries became frustrated with a lack of progress in negotiations over rich countries' agricultural subsidies and other development issues. A 2005 meeting in Hong Kong suffered similar deadlock in negotiations, and the Doha round of talks completely collapsed at a July 2006 meeting in Geneva, Switzerland, largely as a result of continuing disagreements about farm subsidies and tariffs.

In 2008, some experts believe that there is renewed hope for a Doha trade agreement. According to Pascal Lamy, director-general of the WTO, African countries may now be able to convince the United States, the European Union, and Japan to reduce both their farm subsidies and their tariffs on agricultural imports. In return, some of the more developed African nations such as South Africa, Egypt, Tunisia, and Morocco will have to remove some of their tariffs on industrial imports. Such a deal would benefit much of Africa, Lamy says, because many poor countries with farm economies would be able to increase their agricultural exports.

On the other hand, many other commentators see the Doha prospects as still very bleak, and unlikely to produce a workable agreement between developing and developed countries in the near future. The biggest obstacle, doubters say, is the still unresolved impasse over ending agricultural subsidies in rich countries. Also, changes in the political climate and leadership in the United States, one of the most crucial countries involved in the Doha talks, could derail negotiations once again. In addition, experts say, new fears about a possible worldwide economic recession might increase many countries' reluctance to change trading rules and cause them to become more, rather than less, protectionist.

The authors of the viewpoints in this chapter discuss the issues of the need for changes in global trade rules, whether developing African countries should first strengthen their economies before exposing them to worldwide competition, and whether trade will ultimately help or hurt African nations.

Trade Is the Best Type of Aid for Africa

Christa Bieker

Christa Bieker is a policy analyst with the National Center for Policy Analysis, a public policy research organization.

The 48 countries south of the Sahara desert in Africa make up the most impoverished and diseased region of the world. Although wealthy countries have poured more than $450 billion of development assistance into the region since 1980, nearly half the population lives on less than $1 per day, the average life expectancy is only 46 years and nearly one-third of children are underweight and malnourished. Despite its noble intent, aid has not rescued Sub-Saharan Africa from poverty. In many cases, it has undermined development, propped up dictators and fueled corruption.

Historically, development aid has not lifted Africa out of poverty, nor is it likely to do so in the future.

On the other hand, trade has long been a powerful engine of economic growth. Unfortunately, U.S. agricultural policies undermine Africa's economic growth. U.S. farm subsidies encourage over-production, and exports of surplus crops artificially depress world prices. In addition, because tariffs on imports of some African agricultural products are as high as 150 percent, African farmers are often unable to compete in the American market, even if their production costs are lower.

Reducing U.S. trade barriers and farm subsidies would spur growth in Africa. . . .

Christa Bieker, "Trade Is the Best Aid for Africa," *Conservative Colloquium*, National Center for Policy Analysis, September 24, 2007. Reproduced by permission.

The Failure of Foreign Aid

Since 1980, the United States has given more than $40 billion in development assistance to Sub-Saharan Africa. In recent years, public figures ranging from former President Bill Clinton to the rock group U2's Bono have called for even more aid. In 2004, President [George W.] Bush doubled development assistance to Sub-Saharan Africa to $19 billion over 5 years and recently requested an additional $30 billion over 5 years beginning in 2009.

Historically, development aid has not lifted Africa out of poverty, nor is it likely to do so in the future. The average growth in per capita gross domestic product (GDP) in Sub-Saharan Africa from 1980 to 2004 was less than one percent (0.33 percent)! Thus, many of these countries are economically worse off than they were at the end of the colonial era in the 1960s. In fact, foreign aid has often been an obstacle to development.

Aid Creates Dependence

Foreign aid undermines internal reforms. If a country receives a steady income from the outside, it has little motivation to improve from within. Government officials have less incentive to institute macro-economic reforms when the amount of money available for the government to spend doesn't depend on the performance of the economy.

Aid Fuels Corruption. Foreign aid often fails to reach its intended recipients and instead props up corrupt dictators. Transparency International, an organization that fights corruption on a global scale, consistently ranks Sub-Saharan African countries among the governments with the highest levels of corruption worldwide. For example, in Ghana, where corruption is particularly rampant, 80 percent of donor funds are diverted from their intended purpose, often ending up in bank accounts in the West!

Aid Undermines Markets. Government-to-government aid often consists of surplus commodities and money that is earmarked to purchase goods from the donor country. This is particularly true of the United States. Due to price supports and production subsidies, U.S. farmers produce much more than Americans can consume. The government ends up with the surplus and donates it to poor countries. In donee countries, this has caused markets for locally grown farm products to collapse. For subsistence farmers who depend on sales of their crops to purchase all their other needs, markets flooded with free donated food can be devastating. For example, foreign food aid in Tanzania caused many local farmers to abandon their fields.

Trade, Not Aid

Throughout history trade has led to greater productivity and economic growth. Open markets allow countries, companies and regions to specialize in the production of what they do best and import products that can be made more efficiently elsewhere. Economists Jeffery Sachs and Andrew Warner examined trade policies of 117 countries over 20 years and found a strong, positive correlation between free trade and growth. In fact, growth was three to six times higher in open economies than in closed ones.

In many cases the negative economic impact of agricultural subsidies is greater on African countries than the development aid they receive.

Unfortunately, the United States discourages freer international trade through its policy of agricultural protection. U.S. subsidies to farmers have reached staggering levels: In 2006 alone, farm subsidies amounted to $19 billion. Attempts to limit subsidies—beginning with the Freedom to Farm Act of 1996—have not been successful; over the past 10 years taxpayers have spent more than $150 billion on farm subsidies. From 1999 to 2005, U.S. cotton farmers received 86 cents in subsidies for every dollar they received from sales.

Protectionist policies are especially devastating to Sub-Saharan Africa because farming accounts for nearly 70 percent of total employment and is the main source of income for the majority of Africans living in poverty. For example, more than 10 million Africans depend directly on cotton production. Since the 1990s, world cotton prices have fallen by half, much of which is due to U.S. farm subsidies, according to the International Cotton Advisory Committee. Their estimates suggest that world cotton prices would rise by 26 percent if the United States repealed cotton subsidies. This amounts to an increase of over $300 million per year in income for African cotton farmers.

In many cases the negative economic impact of agricultural subsidies is greater on African countries than the development aid they receive. For example, in 2002: [the West African country of] Burkina Faso received $10 million in U.S. aid, yet lost $13.7 million in export earnings due to depressed cotton prices. Chad received $5.7 million in U.S. aid but lost nearly the same amount in export earnings. Togo received $4 million in U.S. aid but lost $7.4 million in export earnings.

In addition to farm subsidies, the United States imposes high tariffs on agricultural products from developing countries. The average tariff on agricultural imports is 18 percent, much higher than the 5 percent average tariff on other imports. In addition, the United States imposes much higher tariffs on the importation of large quantities of certain goods. For example, tariffs on groundnuts, an import that provides income to more than 1 million farmers in Senegal, are as high as 150 percent.

Even the African Growth and Opportunity Act, a trade deal between the United States and 37 countries in Sub-Saharan Africa, discriminates against Africa by excluding dairy products, soft drinks, cocoa, coffee, tea, tobacco, groundnuts and many types of fabrics. Researchers at the World Bank, the International Monetary Fund and the University of Maryland found that Africa will realize less than one-third of the economic benefit the Act would have provided if it were comprehensive and unconditional.

Subsidies No Benefit to United States

U.S. agricultural subsidies not only undermine African development, they do not benefit the United States. Farm subsidies cost taxpayers up to $35 billion annually. Instead of benefiting small family farmers during difficult seasons, most of the subsidies go to the largest farms—nearly three-fourths (72 percent) to the largest 10 percent.

Additionally, tariffs hurt U.S. consumers by raising food prices. For example, due to tariffs, Americans pay about twice as much for sugar as people in other countries, costing American consumers about $1.9 billion annually, according to the Government Accountability Office.

The 2002 Farm Bill expire[d] in September 2007 [but Congress extended it]. Congress [now is] ... deciding what programs to extend, revise, eliminate or add. To enhance economic growth in Africa and save the United States and its taxpayers money, Congress should reduce agricultural subsidies in the [next] Farm Bill.

Africa Needs Trade Not Aid

Bhuwan Thapaliya

Bhuwan Thapaliya is a Nepalese economist, author, analyst, poet, and journalist who is associate editor of the Global Politician, *an independent journal of politics and world affairs.*

During the Cold War much of Africa became a battle-ground for the Superpowers [the United States and the Soviet Union], and there has been a tendency to see the continent as little more than a consumer of endless charity. But the new Africa demands a new attitude from the rich world, as it begins to see itself not as aid-addicted but as a system of emerging markets, capable by their own efforts of profiting from the free flow of trade in the global economy. What is little noticed by the rest of the world is that much of Africa is in the midst of an economic revolution. Though poor by global standards, there is a good chance for Africa to forge its own future.

The best thing that America and Europe can do for Africa is not to give it handouts but to reduce trade barriers and buy [African] products.

The ideal of the rule of law and the concept that lasting prosperity demands stable government have taken hold almost everywhere, and most African governments, moreover, have adopted promising economic policies. Though actions still don't match intentions, developing economic gaps are closing in much of the continent.

Views of Africa Must Change

Africa still needs Western help, but the rich world must stop asking, "What can we do about Africa?" but rather "How do

Bhuwan Thapaliya, "Trade, Not Aid for Africa," *Global Politician*, December 19, 2005. Copyright © 2004–2008 *Global Politician*. Reproduced by permission. www. globalpolitician.com/print.asp?id=1500.

we respond to those African countries that are making real progress and encourage others to do likewise for the benefit of the whole world order?"

The best thing that America and Europe can do for Africa is not to give it handouts but to reduce trade barriers and buy the products that Africa is capable of producing competitively—not just agricultural products but also labor-intensive manufactured goods such as textiles, among others.

But ironically, the rich world order now continues not only to obstruct such imports but also distorts Africa's own markets by using them as a dumping ground for its own subsidized farm products. The rich world must open its markets to textiles from Africa's reforming economies if it really wants to curb African poverty.

The rich world order should concentrate on helping Africa through trade.

The rich world order must furthermore help Africa to sail its own economic boat. Africa receives billions of dollars a year in official assistance, yet, paradoxically, this seems not to have gone to the neediest countries. There is something to be said for giving a lot of assistance to countries taking the lead in making reforms, but the rich world has also at some point to acknowledge that much aid to countries whose governments are lagging in this regard has been wasted.

It is an open secret that foreign investment will do more than a decade's worth of efforts by the International Monetary Fund (IMF) and the World Bank to spur on Africa's laggards. Yet the rich world order faces aid dilemmas. That is why it must become more selective in giving aid and tougher in the manner of delivery. Donors should want to spend their aid for outcomes that can be easily checked and measured.

Helping Africa Through Trade

Nevertheless, the rich world order should concentrate on helping Africa through trade. As a result, large parts of Africa will narrow the income gap between them and richer nations. If enough goes right in the course of Africa's growth, its share of world output will rise markedly.

Africa's prospects are bright, in part because geography no longer poses insuperable obstacles. Africa has the trade routes and the potential to industrialize through export-oriented manufactures, but it still faces many formidable difficulties.

To join the global economy, for instance, African nations must cut tariffs. These taxes, however, are often a vital source of revenue. In such a situation temporary balance-of-payments support, together with generous debt relief, makes sense.

The high incidence of infectious disease in tropical Africa may also fundamentally undermine chances there for rapid economic development. Nonetheless, with time, information technology and medicines will give Africa new opportunities to participate in the global economy.

Let us not forget that modern Africa is development-minded. It is in a state of revolt against poverty and disease. Its aspirations, indeed, are no longer domestic but regional and potentially global. It aspires to social and economic progress based on the optimistic conviction that it, too, can move forward by leaps, as have the rich nations of the West.

Trade Liberalization Has Hurt Poor African Nations

Claire Melamed

Claire Melamed, formerly a trade policy adviser for Christian Aid, now works for Action Aid, a global antipoverty agency.

Trade liberalisation has cost sub-Saharan Africa US$272 billion over the past 20 years. Had they not been forced to liberalise as the price of aid, loans and debt relief, sub-Saharan African countries would have had enough extra income to wipe out their debts and have sufficient left over to pay for every child to be vaccinated and go to school.

Two decades of liberalisation has cost sub-Saharan Africa roughly what it has received in aid. Effectively, this aid did no more than compensate African countries for the losses they sustained by meeting the conditions that were attached to the aid they received. And these losses dwarf the US$40 billion worth of debt relief agreed at the [2005] meeting of G7 finance ministers. [The G7 comprises the United States, the United Kingdom, France, Germany, Italy, Japan, and Canada.]

> *[Liberalisation] results in quantifiable losses in income for some of the poorest countries in the world.*

If new aid and debt relief comes with strings attached that require countries to liberalise trade, it may well do more harm than good. . . .

Free Trade Wreaks Havoc on Africa

Supporters of liberalisation . . . claim that the majority benefit from the new opportunities created by liberalisation. In this briefing, Christian Aid [a non-profit aid group] shows that

Claire Melamed, "The Economics of Failure: The Real Cost of 'Free' Trade for Poor Countries," Christian Aid, June 2005. Reproduced by permission. www.africafocus.org/docs05/trad0507.php.

this is not the case. Complementing our previous case studies, which show the devastation trade liberalisation wreaks on individuals, we demonstrate that whole countries would be much richer today if they had not been forced to open their markets.

Christian Aid commissioned an expert in econometrics to work out what might have happened had trade not been liberalised, using economic modelling. The work was reviewed by a panel of academics. The model looked at what trade liberalisation has meant for 32 countries, most in Africa but some in Asia and Latin America.

The data came from [international organizations such as] the World Bank, International Monetary Fund [IMF], United Nations and academic studies. We established the year each country began to liberalise and the extent of its trade liberalisation. We used evidence on the impact of trade liberalisation on imports and exports, and the effect of this on national income, to estimate how much income was lost given the extent of liberalisation. The results suggested that:

- imports tend to rise faster than exports following trade liberalisation

- this results in quantifiable losses in income for some of the poorest countries in the world.

We are not arguing that countries which liberalise do not grow, or that some people in them do not become less poor but we are saying that without liberalisation, growth could have been higher and poverty reduction faster.

This report shows the true cost of the policies that have been forced on the developing world by donor countries and international institutions. The devastation import liberalisation has caused agricultural and industrial production in developing countries and the way it has severely limited their prospects of future development is well documented. This report puts a value on that loss.

The Price of Liberalisation

When trade is liberalised, imports climb steeply as new products flood in. Local producers are priced out of their markets by new, cheaper, better-marketed goods. Exports also tend to grow, but not by as much. Demand for the kind of things sub-Saharan African countries tend to export such as raw materials doesn't change much, so there isn't a lot of scope for increasing exports. This means that, overall, local producers are selling less than they were before trade was liberalised.

There are more poor people in sub-Saharan Africa now than there were 20 years ago.

In the long run, it's production that keeps a country going and if trade liberalisation means reduced production, in the end it will mean lower incomes. Any gains to consumers in the short term will be wiped out in the long term as their incomes fall and unemployment rises.

This has been the story of sub-Saharan Africa over the past 20 years. Trade liberalisation has cost the 22 African countries in the modelling exercise more than US$170 billion in that time. According to our model, this is the amount that the GDP [gross domestic product, a measure of total economic output] of these countries would have increased had they not liberalised their trade in the 1980s and 1990s. If the model is applied to all of sub-Saharan Africa, the loss is US$272 billion.

While some countries in Africa have increased their GDP over the past 20 years, this increase is not as great as it could have been. There are more poor people in sub-Saharan Africa now than there were 20 years ago. Some of them would not be poor today were it not for inappropriate trade liberalisation.

In the year 2000 alone, sub-Saharan Africa lost nearly US$45 dollars per person thanks to trade liberalisation. Most trade liberalisation in Africa has been part of the conditions attached to foreign aid, loans and debt relief. This looks like a bad deal: in 2000, aid per person in sub-Saharan Africa was less than half the loss from liberalisation only US$20. Africa is losing much more than it gains if aid comes with policy strings attached.

The staggering truth is that the US$272 billion liberalisation has cost sub-Saharan Africa would have wiped clean the debt of every country in the region (estimated at US$204 billion) and still left more than enough money to pay for every child to be vaccinated and go to school.

The negative effects of trade liberalisation are not confined to Africa. Low-income countries in Asia and Latin America have suffered similar consequences. The average loss to the countries in Christian Aid's study was about 11 per cent of total GDP over 20 years amounting to several billion dollars for each country. The total loss for the 32 countries in the study was US$896 billion.

How Liberalisation Hurts Poor Nations

Academic studies have shown that the main impact of liberalisation on trade flows is to increase the demand for imports at a faster rate than the demand for exports. That is, following trade liberalisation, countries tend to buy more than they sell every year. As a result, their trade balance worsens and they have to live beyond their means, a situation which is not sustainable in the long term, without constant inflows of ever-increasing aid.

As imports increase, demand in the country for locally produced goods falls, because people are buying imported goods instead. The demand for exports doesn't increase enough to make up for the fall in local demand. For farmers, this will mean producing less, or selling at a lower price. For manufacturers, this might mean going out of business altogether.

As a result, developing countries could become increasingly indebted as they continue to spend more than they earn. However, poorer developing countries are highly unlikely to receive the finance either loans, grants or investment flows to fund this increased expenditure. Africa, for example, has been a net exporter of capital for much of the 1980s and 1990s. Trade and finance liberalisation have been associated with increased capital flight from Africa. The problem has been compounded by reduced aid to Africa during the 1990s.

If more money doesn't come in from elsewhere, as aid, loans or foreign investment, the impact will be felt on GDP in the medium to long term. As demand for their products fails, local producers earn less, the total income of the country declines and imports eventually return to their pre-liberalisation levels all of which leads to a lower level of national income than would be the case without trade liberalisation.

Who Paid the Price?

If a country's GDP falls, it doesn't affect everyone equally. It is often the poor who suffer most. Recent evidence from the United Nations shows that countries which liberalised their trade most tended to suffer from increases in poverty. Countries that cut themselves off from trade altogether don't reduce poverty very successfully either in fact, it was countries with moderate levels of protection that did best.

Anecdotal evidence supports this general trend. Christian Aid has produced numerous case studies over the years which show how poor people have been affected by trade liberalisation.

- Tomato production used to provide rural households in Senegal with a good living. But after liberalisation, the prices farmers received for their tomatoes halved, and tomato production fell from 73,000 tonnes in 1990 to just 20,000 tonnes in 1997, leaving many farmers without a cash crop.

- In Kenya, both cotton farming and textile production have been hit. Cotton production, a key income earner for poor households, fell from 70,000 bales a year in the mid-1980s to less than 20,000 bales in the mid-1990s. Employment in textile factories fell from 120,000 people to 85,000 in just ten years.

- Rice imports in Ghana climbed to 314,626 tonnes per year following trade liberalisation. For local farmers, the results have been catastrophic. One of them told Christian Aid: 'One of the main problems we face is the marketing of our rice. We find it difficult to compete with imported rice on the market.'

As the examples above indicate, it is often poor farmers who suffer most when trade is liberalised. The fall in domestic demand which results from increased imports hits them particularly hard. Poor farmers have little access to capital or technology to increase their productivity or improve the quality of what they sell in response to more competition. They are also competing in an extremely unequal market, where imports from developed countries are often heavily subsidised.

Manufacturing industries have not grown up to employ people who are no longer able to make a living from farming. Instead, manufacturing has also been hard hit by trade liberalisation:

- In Zambia, employment in formal-sector manufacturing fell by 40 per cent in just five years following trade liberalisation.

- In Ghana, employment in manufacturing fell from 78,700 in 1987 to 28,000 in 1993 following trade liberalisation.

- In Malawi, textile production fell by more than half between 1990 and 1996. Many firms manufacturing consumer goods like soap and cooking oils went out of business, and the poultry industry collapsed in the face of cheap imports.

A closer examination of import and export trends following liberalisation shows how this happened. In all the countries for which it had data, the UN Conference on Trade and Development (UNCTAD) found that, following trade liberalisation, imports of food increased as a proportion of all imports, while imports of machinery declined, again as a proportion of all imports. The increase in cheap food imports priced farmers out of local markets. The relative decline in imports of machinery showed that manufacturers were also suffering; importing less machinery to run their factories, improve productivity and provide more jobs.

Trade liberalisation means a 'double whammy' for poor people, stifling the development of industry which would replace lost jobs in agriculture. Wherever they turn, poor people are hard hit by trade liberalisation.

Trade liberalisation is not a good policy.

Export trends bear this out. Though exports did increase in most cases following trade liberalisation, most countries simply exported more of the same, they did not start to export more manufactured goods, for example, or more higher-value agricultural exports. An UNCTAD study also found that many least-developed countries lost market share following trade liberalisation, as their exports failed to compete in international markets.

It is clear that trade liberalisation is not driving the development of a more dynamic, diversified or pro-poor pattern of development. On the contrary, it is locking Africa into greater dependence on a few agricultural products whose prices have been declining for 50 years. Liberalisation is hitting manufacturing hard and it is the development of manufacturing that Africa needs if it is ever to trade its way out of poverty.

Not a Good Policy

Trade liberalisation is not a good policy that has unfortunate consequences for a small minority of people. It is a policy imposed on developing countries by donors and international institutions that has systematically deprived some of the poorest people in the world of opportunities to develop their own economies and end poverty.

Poor people have been driven out of their domestic markets and found no international markets to compensate them. Development has stalled as industries have collapsed and imports of capital goods fallen, exacerbating the crisis in agriculture as fewer employment opportunities are available elsewhere.

African countries have lost hundreds of billions of dollars in 20 years of liberalisation. This means lost opportunities for education, for life-saving medicines and for investment in infrastructure and new industries. Instead, many African countries have seen increases in poverty. Trade liberalisation and those who have forced it on Africa must take its share of the blame.

What Can Be Done?

First, the drive to more liberalisation must stop. G8 countries [the eight largest industrialized countries: Canada, Japan, France, Germany, Italy, Russia, the United States and the United Kingdom] must:

- use their controlling stake in the World Bank and IMF to stop them forcing countries to liberalise trade as a condition of loans, grants and debt relief

- stop forcing countries to liberalise trade as a condition of bilateral aid and debt relief. As a first step, the UK

Free Trade Benefits Developed Countries

Malawi was not rejecting free trade per se. But like other Third World agricultural nations, Malawi has found that free-trade policies that are supposed to help economies develop in fact seem to make subsidized cash crops from developed countries more competitive.

The World Bank says subsidies impede trade; underwriting seed and fertilizer would give Malawian farmers an unfair advantage. And yet American and French farmers, who are regularly subsidized by their governments, sell grain to Malawi. Is that fair competition? Or just plain hypocrisy? Who can blame the cynical for thinking that the International Monetary Fund [IMF] and the World Bank—international institutions dedicated to promoting economic growth and eradicating poverty—manipulate the rules to the benefit of rich nations? The Third World goose marches to the tune of [American economics theorist] Milton Friedman, while the First World gander plugs its ears and lets the subsidies flow.

The free market can contribute to economic development and even provide a basis for greater democracy, but only if the rules apply equally to the wealthy and the poor.

In the end, even U.S. foreign aid gets distorted. According to a report in *The New York Times* [in December 2007], the United States has given Malawi $147 million in food relief since 2002—in essence, an undeclared subsidy to American farmers. But it has given only $53 million to help farmers in Malawi grow their own food. And not a nickel for the fertilizer subsidy program.

There are countless examples of the pernicious effect of donor hypocrisy. Argentina played by the IMF's rules, dismantling much of its social agenda as instructed, yet reaped not prosperity but the whirlwind [disaster]. Not so long ago, ore-rich regions of Africa allowed the World Bank to pump money into mining and other extraction industries, and watched investors walk away with all the profits. The World Bank has since changed its tune, but the damage has been done.

Investors talk about "conditionality," meaning recipient nations must hew the free-market line to secure capital investment, even if that means cutting healthcare, food subsidies, social insurance and other popular government benefits. Only by challenging such market nostrums did Malawi's political leaders preempt potentially catastrophic economic and political consequences—rural poverty, dependency on foreign food and even famine.

A Threat to Democracy

Malawi found a way out, but the danger elsewhere is that nations fed up with First World hypocrisy will throw democracy out with trade-and-aid rules. Argentina's experience made it easy for other Latin American leaders, such as [Venezuelan president] Hugo Chavez, to be demagogues on free trade and undermine democracy through guilt by association. Chavez— who has consistently thumbed his nose at free-market rules by manipulating the oil industry—tried to leverage discontent with globalization and free trade to eliminate term limits on his presidency and obliterate constraints on presidential power. He came within a percentage point of getting his way in a [2007] vote.

In Iraq, free-market zealotry has contributed to the unfolding anarchy. After Baghdad's fall, U.S. administrators seemed convinced that democratization and privatization were the same thing—that forcing free-market rules on the new government would enhance Iraqi autonomy. It did not, any more than it did in Argentina or Malawi.

The free market can contribute to economic development and even provide a basis for greater democracy, but only if the rules apply equally to the wealthy and the poor. And only if developing nations are permitted enough leeway to help their people (through subsidies, welfare programs or other government interventions) reach a stage at which they are capable of competing with First World economies that have had a century or more head start.

So if bickering U.S. presidential candidates are wondering why the Iraqi economy is in disarray, why Chavez is popular in much of Latin America and why so many people in the developing world see U.S.-led globalization and free trade as a form of servitude, they might take a careful look at Malawi's peaceful and successful economic revolution.

CHAPTER 4

Will Oil and Other Natural Resources Save Africa?

Chapter Preface

Africa is fast becoming a pivotal region in the developing world's search for oil, natural gas, and other natural resources. Although Africa's total proven oil reserves—oil supplies that geological information indicates could be easily recovered—make up only about 7 percent of global oil supply, Africa now accounts for 12 percent of the world's crude oil production. The continent also is quickly increasing its oil reserve estimates and production levels. In fact, according to news reports, one out of every four barrels of oil discovered outside of the United States and Canada between 2000 and 2004 came from Africa, and by 2010 African oil may account for as much as 30 percent of world production.

The rapid growth of Africa's oil market is due to several factors that make it highly desirable. First, African oil is low in sulfur, making it easy to refine and valuable for environmental reasons. African oil reserves are also located in areas that allow the oil to be readily transported to the eastern seaboard of the United States and other oil-hungry countries. Also, in an age of Islamic terrorism, the United States and other Western countries need reliable oil suppliers outside of the volatile Middle East. All these factors have contributed to an oil boom in many African countries, including Angola, Nigeria, Guinea, and Chad.

The United States therefore sees Africa as an important source for future oil supplies. Today in 2008, about 15 percent of U.S. oil imports come from Africa, but by 2010, experts say this could rise to 20 percent. The Council on Foreign Relations estimated that about $20 billion will be invested in African oil by U.S. companies by 2010. By the end of the next decade, the United States may be even more heavily dependent on African oil. Some experts estimate, for example, that 35 percent of U.S. oil imports may eventually come from African countries. The United States, however, is encountering stiff competition for Africa's oil reserves from other countries— mainly China, which has been investing heavily in the region.

Because of the significance of Africa's oil to U.S. consumers, the threat posed by China's advances in the region, and the desire to ensure that radical Islamic terrorism does not spread into oil-rich African countries, the continent is now considered to be strategically important to the United States government and military. Many commentators suggest that this strategic importance is the real reason behind America's recent aid increases to the region. In addition, to protect strategic U.S. oil interests and counter the Chinese threat, the U.S. military is reorganizing its command structure and establishing a new unified command for the area under the name AFRICOM. Former secretary of defense Donald Rumsfeld began planning for the new command in 2006, and it was formally announced by President George W. Bush in 2007 and became operational in 2008. General William Ward, a four-star African-American general, was named AFRICOM's first commander.

The Bush administration has sought to portray the new military command as a partnership with African nations that will seek to promote mutual interests. As the White House said in a February 6, 2007, press release, AFRICOM "will enhance our efforts to bring peace and security to the people of Africa and promote our common goals of development, health, education, democracy, and economic growth in Africa." However, skeptics—many of them Africans—worry that the new U.S. interest in the continent is really part of a dangerous international scramble for Africa's resources that may militarize Africa and produce little benefit for poor Africans. Commentators have expressed concerns, for example, that a new Cold War may develop in Africa between China and the United States, in which each country will use African nations as pawns or will provide arms and aid to one faction or another, thereby destabilizing the region further and promoting more violence and conflict. In fact, at least for now, AFRICOM will be headquartered in Germany, partly due to unexpected resistance by African nations to the establishment of U.S. military bases in Africa.

Critics have urged that U.S. policy toward Africa should be redirected away from the AFRICOM-type military presence and toward debt cancellation, fair trade policies, and increased development assistance focused on local solutions that could build sustainable communities and give Africans a sense of independence and self-determination. This policy of self-determination would also allow Africa to settle its own civil wars and terrorist threats. Critics say precedent has already been set for this in the 1990s when the Economic Community of West African States set up an armed Monitoring Group (Ecomog) to respond to the civil war in Liberia. Ecomog helped to drive rebels out of the capital and kept Liberia from disintegrating.

Whether African nations can use their oil reserves for good and resist what for many other oil-rich nations has been the curse of oil wealth remains to be seen. The viewpoints in this chapter address the critical question of what impact Africa's oil and other valuable natural resources will have on African hopes for development and autonomy.

Selling Natural Resources to China Is Helping African Economic Development

Eliza Barclay

Eliza Barclay is a writer based in Washington, D.C., who reports on Latin America and Africa.

Inside a dark shop opposite a frenetic bus station, transistor radios are stacked beneath newfangled LED flashlights, and belts hang like snakes from the ceiling, their buckles emblazoned with the decidedly un-African word *Guangzhou* [a city in China]. Outside, in the equatorial sunshine, men who crowded inside the store become mobile versions of it, strapping to their backs 4-foot-wide square racks interlaced with watches, wallets, belts, and other items.

A lanky young vendor whom I'll call Charles walks miles to the city's outskirts shouldering a weighty rack of trinkets, hoping to unload it along the way. Charles, who asked that his real name not be used because it's illegal to vend in the city center, hawks plastic watches for 40 cents and leather belts for $1.80, but his sales are consistent, and on a good day he takes home $45 in earnings. What is impressive about Charles' operation is not only the low, low prices of the Chinese goods he sells but that he brings them to people in the slums who've never bought these things before.

"These new Chinese products help low-income people because they can't afford the European or American stuff," says Mr. Abasi, who owns the store that supplies Charles and other vendors. "People know these products are not good quality, but they buy them because they look expensive."

Eliza Barclay, "Trade-Offs: Is China the Key to Africa's Development?" *Slate*, March 6, 2008. Copyright © 2008 Washingtonpost.Newsweek International. Reproduced by permission of the author. www.slate.com/id/2185853/pagenum/all/#page_start.

Rising Chinese Investment

While the United States and Europe still loom large here as cultural and economic icons, China is making inroads into Africa in rivulets. In this city, Tanzania's second largest, the rivulets take the form of manufactured goods, construction projects like roads and cellphone towers, and a smattering of Chinese restaurants. For a desperately poor country like Tanzania, this "South-South" trade with China has created massive new opportunities for accelerating economic development.

In recent years, the increase in trade flows between sub-Saharan Africa and Asia has been dramatical—exports from Asia to Africa have grown at an annual rate of 18 percent since 2002. Part of the equation is that low-cost goods from China fit economies like Tanzania's well. Goods like those sold by Charles are low-quality and sometimes fake, but they are creating new microenterprise opportunities for entrepreneurial Africans. Charles told me he, like many other Arusha vendors who had regular jobs before going independent, worked in a shoe shop until he was laid off.

The new opportunities to trade with China are so tantalizing for Africans that some are returning from abroad to invest in their homelands. Georgine Spake is an elegant, tall Congolese woman who speaks English with a thick French accent and lives in the leafy suburbs of Washington, D.C., with her American husband and four children. Upon visiting her birthplace of Kinshasa [in] June [2007], after a nine-year hiatus, Spake told me she was dumbfounded to discover that most of her friends and family were traveling to and from China to do business. Lured by the promise of mining her own respectable profit, Spake flew to the bustling manufacturing hub of Guangzhou, China, to investigate import opportunities with a cousin who was already importing security cameras and telephones. She stayed for a month, paying a Congolese man who lived there $150 to be her translator and fixer throughout her stay. By the end, she arranged for the shipment of 30 tons of garlic to be sold at wholesale in Kinshasa. She chose garlic, she said, because there has been great demand for it since the eastern Democratic Republic of Congo [DRC], which traditionally cultivated garlic and onions, fell prey to conflict.

China is discovering Tanzania's natural resources. . . . Chinese companies are buying millions of dollars' worth of indigenous hardwood logs.

According to Spake, Guangzhou was swarming with Africans. Each night, many of them congregated at a bar called the Elephant, where African musicians and dancers performed. There she exchanged business tips in hushed tones with Senegalese, Cameroonians, and Zimbabweans, as their local handlers hovered nearby to prevent their clients from being poached by other handlers.

Spake now communicates with a Chinese partner by e-mail and phone and plans to return to Guangzhou to arrange more shipments of garlic and, perhaps, tomato paste.

Though the trade balance between China and Africa is heavily weighted toward Chinese exports, Africa's exports to China grew by 48 percent annually between 1999 and 2004, according to the World Bank. Just as it has grown ravenous for Sudan's oil and the DRC's gold, China is discovering Tanzania's natural resources. In the southern coastal region, Chinese companies are buying millions of dollars' worth of indigenous hardwood logs to feed China's construction and furniture industries, which supply companies like IKEA with products. Nonprofit organizations that monitor the trade in illicit goods have tracked the flow of ivory from and through Tanzania to China.

The Downside of Trade with China

But as China's investments grow increasingly hard to resist, the fast-flowing trade is ripe for corruption in weak African states like Tanzania. A report released in May 2007 by TRAF-FIC International, a joint program of the WWF [World Wildlife Fund] and IUCN [International Union for the Conservation of Nature]—the World Conservation Union, found that Tanzania had lost $58 million in timber revenue to corruption, in part because the majority of the timber sales were illegal. Most of the benefits from the trade were lumped among a select few groups with little trickling down to the communities living closest to the forests.

China is giving the African people a chance to do business and make more money, and for some people that means being able to buy food to eat.

One way to ensure that local communities benefit from the logging is to process timber products on African soil before exporting them, says Rogers Malimbwi, a professor of natural resources at Sokoine University in Dar es Salaam. Tanzania's timber sector is beginning to build mills to process the timber, but much of it still leaves the country as intact logs, he said.

Meanwhile, African consumers are also beginning to experience the ugly side of trading with China, a lesson Americans learned all too well [in 2007] with the massive recalls of Chinese-made dog food and toys. In October 2007, counterfeit electrical equipment from China caused fatal electrical fires in Dar es Salaam, the country's commercial capital, according to the Confederation of Tanzania Industries, which called for a crackdown on counterfeits.

"The Chinese medicines are making people sick, and the electrical wires are not safe," said Spake. "But China is giving the African people a chance to do business and make more money, and for some people that means being able to buy food to eat."

Oil Resources May Give Africa a Great Chance to Develop

Institute for the Analysis of Global Security

The Institute for the Analysis of Global Security is a nonprofit educational organization focused on energy security.

Although not all OPEC [Organization of Petroleum Exporting Countries] countries are corrupt, an historical symbiosis exists between oil and corruption. Oil, corruption and failed states seem to be synonymous. However, some countries have been able to address this threat; most of them are located in North Africa. Producing countries such as Algeria, Egypt, Tunisia and even in some respects Libya, have managed to resist the temptation of sleaze. While temptation may have been countered by most North African producers, the threat of falling into the same trap remains.

Oil (and increasingly natural gas) is both the greatest strength and the biggest weakness of the North African region. As has been obvious for decades, revenues generated by these two hydrocarbon based resources still account for the vast bulk of economic activity, particularly in Algeria and Libya. The oil windfall has prevented the development of more broad-based economies and has created an industry that does not require mass employment.

However, the revenues of a hydrocarbon based economy are not exceptionally well equipped to support sustainable and supra-sectoral economic growth. While the growing importance of the gas sector in recent years has provided a welcome element of diversification, it too fails to provide the jobs that the people of North Africa seek.

Institute for the Analysis of Global Security, "Will North Africa Learn from the Oil Curse?" *Energy Security*, January 24, 2005. Copyright © 2004 Institute for the Analysis of Global Security. All rights reserved. Reproduced by permission. www.iags.org/ n0124053.htm.

To some extent, oil revenues drive the economies of all parts of the Middle East and North Africa (MENA) region. While the biggest oil producers are concentrated in the [Persian] Gulf, North African states such as Algeria and Libya are heavily dependent upon oil income. Even modest producers such as Egypt rely on oil output to generate export revenues, while Tunisia's limited oil production allows the country to avoid a heavy fuel import bill. At the same time, much of the investment in the region's non-oil producers is provided by companies and financial institutions based in hydrocarbon-rich states which have benefited from oil revenues.

Current high crude oil prices, which additionally have had their positive implications for natural gas exports too, have brought oil revenue of almost unknown historical levels. . . . In contrast to prior decades, most of the massive surplus will undoubtedly be channelled into other investment sectors, such as power, infrastructure and immense construction projects. Some producers also operate special oil funds to act as a counterweight to fluctuating prices (excess revenues are paid in when prices are high and can be drawn upon when prices are depressed.) Yet if prices remain high, new investment funds are certain to be made available.

Some North African countries may reap additional rewards from the current crude oil prices.

Still, one major economic fact of life has not been learned yet. State-run or owned enterprises are counterproductive in setting up a new and competitive economy. State-dominated economies have intrinsic and very dangerous weaknesses. [Non-diversification] . . . in most Gulf based economies, except maybe Dubai . . . is still a fact of life, and is not producing the targeted results at all.

State control does permit the cross subsidisation of surplus oil profits from hydrocarbon parastatals [state-owned or

-subsidized oil companies] to other ventures. If the current oil boom is sustained, or even if prices merely remain above the US$30 per barrel level, further investment in oilfield development is likely. When prices remained within OPEC's US$22–28 basket range, most Middle Eastern members of the oil cartel possessed excess production capacity that was not being utilised. This obviously depressed investment in exploration and the development of new fields. Now most are producing at full capacity and so both private and state-owned oil companies will be keen to bring online new fields in order to reap the benefits of high oil prices.

Future Rewards

Some North African countries may reap additional rewards from the current crude oil prices. High prices make it increasingly profitable to develop the large amount of marginal fields, where production costs are high, such as onshore Western Desert, Egypt, or even Morocco's mountain range reserves. Most of North Africa's immense reserves with low production costs are concentrated in two countries: Algeria and Libya. With higher crude oil prices, the other Arabic-speaking countries will be able to compete with Siberia, Nigeria, Sao Tome & Principe, Angola or even Sudan, in attracting increased foreign direct investment for infrastructure in the near future. The growing discrepancies between the OPEC producers claimed reserves—largely based on state provided figures—and true levels may also begin to play a major role.

North Africa has been given a great chance to secure its future. Let us hope the governments in the region will not squander it.

In contrast to Persian Gulf-based producers, North Africa has become an oasis of transparency. The current North African regimes have been able to address the necessary changes in their state-run economies needed to attract the international investment that is so badly needed. The enormous accounting scandals in the West (Enron, WorldCom) have shaken the investment sectors on Wall Street and London City, and the call for transparency and accountability has resonated within the oil sector as well. The immense reserve debacle of Royal Dutch/Shell, the Russian oil farce surrounding Yukos and other events have pushed forward increased openness worldwide. Investors and operators, forced by their shareholders and institutional investors will ask for more transparency before investments are granted. North African countries have heard the message and acted accordingly. Algeria, Egypt, Tunisia and even Libya, are leading the way in this respect. Saudi Arabia's unwillingness to open its reserve archives and databanks for international scrutiny could become a blessing to North African producers.

A Chance for Development

The fear among analysts is that of renewed rentierism; that is, an economy based on revenues from natural resources without more diversified income sources. It is hoped that Libya and Algeria have learned from past mistakes. While petroleum based revenue sources will be a major part of their economies for decades, the role of the sector should change. Rentierism should not figure in governmental strategy. Revenues should be used for diversification, not only to strengthen the overall economic basis of a country but also to establish the means by which employment can be increased. The immense population booms experienced in countries such as Egypt, where there are more children born every year than official employment figures are able to cope with, is undermining the economic situation. As long as oil producing countries are struggling to keep up GDP [gross domestic product] per capita, even during high revenue scenarios, worrying times are ahead.

International operators and investors have a role to play in addressing these issues, not only in developing the communities in which they are working but also preventing unwanted socio-economic effects from generating conflict on a suprar-egional level. The call for the end of rentier states, especially in North Africa, is based on two premises: the development of local economies and the stabilisation of the respective regions. North Africa has been given a great chance to secure its future. Let us hope the governments in the region will not squander it.

Corrupt Leaders Are Squandering Africa's Natural Resources

Thilo Thielke

Thilo Thielke is the Africa correspondent for Der Spiegel, *a German newsmagazine.*

The Americans and the Chinese are vying for control of Africa's huge oil reserves. China's growing industrial base is also foraging for copper, manganese and tropical hardwood to feed its voracious appetite. Africa's dictators are the real winners.

Dokubo-Asari, who has given himself the terrifying first name of Mujahid, had no way of anticipating his imminent arrest. The beefy rebel leader plunged thick fingers into his bowl, fished out a fatty piece of chicken from the sauce, and shoved it into his mouth, dripping a red trail on his white caftan in the process. Smacking his lips, he launched into tales of his exploits.

The Niger Delta could not be compared with Bosnia, at least not yet, he expounded with a touch of pride. After all, he could already mobilize more than 100,000 troops. If the government continued to betray him, he would unleash this force, targeting the governor's bandits, the oil companies—and all foreigners.

Of the approximately 130 gangs, which go by names such as "The Vikings," "The Icelanders," the "National Alliance of Adventurers" and "Black Ax," the 41-year-old Dokubo-Asari

Thilo Thielke, "The Race for Resources: Gangsters and Africa's Black Gold Rush," *Spiegel Online*, December 7, 2005. Copyright © 2005 Spiegel Online. Reproduced by permission. www.spiegel.de/international/spiegel/0,1518,389138,00.html.

may well command the toughest of the bunch: a band of warriors from the Ijaw tribe that has its home in the delta. His militia is suspected of regularly tapping Shell's pipelines, kidnapping or killing its workers, and staging shootouts with rivals on the streets. The BBC [British Broadcasting Corporation] estimates that Dokubo-Asari has some 2,000 desperados under his control. He has christened his guerilla fighters with the ostentatious title "Niger Delta People's Volunteer Force."

The havoc these renegades can wreak is all too familiar to Royal Dutch Shell, which pumps one million barrels of oil a day in Nigeria. According to its annual report, an average of 50,000 barrels a day were stolen in 2004, at a loss of almost $1 billion. In the same period, a dozen workers were killed, between 50 and 70 kidnapped, and a total of 314 criminal incidents recorded. Pumping had to be halted 176 times. A complete tanker, the *African Pride*, even disappeared, ne'er to be seen again!

Fossil fuel has allegedly brought more than $280 billion dollars into Nigeria. Most of this has disappeared into the pockets of corrupt politicians.

"The oil theft is bleeding us white," company spokesman Larry Ossai complains in Nigeria's capital, Abuja. For the security company WAC Global Services, conditions in the Niger Delta may even recall Chechnya [a region of civil war in Russia]. . . .

[In 2005], Nigerian officials decided enough was enough. Dokubo-Asari was taken into custody on charges of planning a coup. Since then the conflict has been threatening to careen out of control. One hundred heavily armed Dokubo supporters seized an oil rig operated by Chevron. As a precaution, the American oil company shut down a second platform. Shell too has pulled out workers. . . .

The Lure of African Oil

[However,] no other place in the world is currently discovering oil reserves as fast as Africa's terra incognita [unknown land]. Already, some 8 million barrels are being pumped every day. High-quality crude, light and low in sulfur. Easily processed into gasoline, African oil is in high demand.

In the past three decades alone, fossil fuel has allegedly brought more than $280 billion dollars into Nigeria. Most of this has disappeared into the pockets of corrupt politicians. The *Economist* has referred to a recently concluded debt relief program for the resource-rich country as "laughable." There is every indication that the cash will keep flowing. The oil industry predators have been circling the chaotic countries located on the Gulf of Guinea in increasing numbers—not just as a result of the stratospheric rise in oil prices and dwindling reserves in the other [that is, the Persian] Gulf.

Up to 100 billion barrels are thought to be hidden, primarily off the West African coast—roughly the equivalent of Iraq's reserves. U.S. congressman William Jefferson announced happily in 2004: "Last year, 8 billion barrels of oil were discovered around the world, and seven billion of them were off the West African coast." The treasure trove is there for the taking.

Dizzying Growth Rates

The United States has a particular interest in these reserves: Nigeria is its fifth largest supplier of crude, with central and western Africa making up 15 percent of its oil imports. That figure will soon hit 20 percent.

Dizzying growth rates are projected for countries like Nigeria and Angola, where corruption is endemic. In the not-too-distant future, they could even double their output. The inflow of cash is expected to reach tidal proportions across the Gulf of Guinea: in Gabon, Congo-Brazzaville, Equatorial Guinea, Sao Tome and Principe. The oilfields extend hundreds of miles inland.

Massive pipelines are already channeling crude from Chad to the western coast. From there, a tanker can reach Texas in half the time it takes from the Persian Gulf. The next country on the drilling schedule is Cameroon. "Within the next five years, the region will be adding two to three million barrels per day to the world market," the Center for Strategic and International Studies forecasts: "a full 20 percent of the new production capacity worldwide." Experts predict[ed] that the eight biggest oil-producing countries in Africa [earned] $35 billion in 2005 alone.

Geologist Tom Windle, who tracked down oil reserves in West Africa for Amoco, thinks eastern Africa has the most potential: "If someone came to me and said, 'Here's a billion dollars; I want you to open up a new frontier basin,' I would say, 'Right, the East African margin.'" Exxon Mobil, Woodside Petroleum and Tullow Oil are already at work in the continent's east. In Somalia, the hunt was halted in 1991 by the country's devastating civil war. But with a new government elected in the fall of 2004, the oil companies' representatives have been flocking to its provisional capital in Jowhar.

"Africa Holds All the Aces"

A huge pan-African oil field extends from Port Sudan to Port Harcourt—with a special attraction: With the exception of Nigeria, no African country south of the Sahara is a member of OPEC [Organization of Petroleum Exporting Countries]. And Nigeria itself continues to toy with the notion of quitting the cartel, enabling it to boost production to 4 million barrels a day by 2010.

African muscle would seem the only way to ease the Arab world's stranglehold on prices. It is no wonder that Washington considers West Africa one of the American market's fastest growing sources for oil and gas.

That, at last, is good news for a continent best known for its suffering. And the news is getting better still: China too has discovered Africa's potential as a supplier. The emerging economic superpower desperately needs natural resources to maintain its annual 9 percent growth rate.

Never before have the United States and China been so focused on Africa, and their interest will only grow keener. The battle for the black gold has already begun. "Africa holds all the aces," the magazine *Africa Today* says.

The Chinese evidently have few scruples. After the United States declared Islamic-governed Sudan a rogue state for harboring Osama Bin Laden, forcing the American companies to abandon their lucrative trade with the country's crude, China was only too happy to fill the void. Today China is a major investor in the land of the Mahdi [Islamic messiah]. In return, Sudan ships 60 percent of its oil to the Asian power—not exactly peanuts, given its daily output of 340,000 barrels. Once the Melut oil field comes on line in the near future, the total could rise to 800,000 barrels a day.

Instead of compelling the Africans to embrace democracy and transparency, [China defends]. . . authoritarian African leaders who have been rebuffed by the West.

The Chinese view their commitment to Sudan as a long-term partnership. Just recently, an army of Chinese workers began building a second, 1,500 kilometer pipeline from its southern oil fields to Port Sudan on the Red Sea. In the quid pro quo deal, [Sudan's] Umar Al Bashir's government—which invests almost two-thirds of its oil revenues in its military—will be supplied with weapons from the People's Republic [of China]: armaments it desperately needs to wage war in its eastern provinces and against the rebels in Darfur.

China Looks to Profit from Genocide

It is no surprise that the Chinese government knows how to reward such constructive cooperation. Whenever harsh resolutions against the mass murderers in [Sudan's capital of] Khartoum have been tabled at the UN China has stood ready to wield its veto. As [then] U.S. secretary of state, Colin Powell was quick to condemn the slaughter in Darfur as genocide. But China's ambassador to the U.S., Zhou Wenzhong, takes a different view of his country's actions. "Business is business," he maintains. "The situation in Sudan is an internal matter." Now a frustrated United States is resigned to watching Beijing torpedo its security and human rights strategies. What is more, it is powerless to stop China from securing control of Sudan's oil reserves. China already gets 6 percent of its crude from Sudan, on a par with its imports from Russia.

"We import oil from every source we can get it from," admits Li Xiaobing, deputy director of the West Asia and Africa Department in China's Ministry of Trade.

For German political scientist Denis Tull—who compiled a report entitled "The People's Republic of China's Approach to Africa"—China's growing political influence in Africa is "generally negative."

Instead of compelling the Africans to embrace democracy and transparency, Beijing's vehement "defense of the principle of sovereignty" was instead benefiting authoritarian African leaders who have been rebuffed by the West, Tull says.

Zimbabwean President Robert Mugabe . . . authorized the Chinese to exploit platinum deposits in his ailing country—and received military aircraft worth $100 million.

Their hands tied, EU [European Union] foreign ministers have watched China's capitalist corps advance across the continent, making a mockery of their attempts to democratize the authoritarian regimes through aid. China already imports over 28 percent of its oil from Africa. Between 1989 and 1997, the volume of trade rose 431 percent. Since then, it has "more than quintupled"—hitting a record $24 billion. Sometime soon, China is expected to displace Great Britain as Africa's third largest trading partner. Of the 40 bilateral investment agreements China signed between 1995 and 2003, 18 were with African countries. By 2004, 700 Chinese companies had descended on the continent's markets; their direct investments totaled $1.5 billion.

China is buying up anything its ravenous industrial sector can consume: wood from Congo, copper from Zambia, and manganese from Gabon for use in steel production. In return, Africa is receiving mass-produced goods made in China. Their affordability makes these commodities particularly attractive to the poor countries south of the Sahara: clothing, transistor radios—and kalashnikovs [assault rifles].

Traffic is heavy in both directions. So much so that Kenya Airways has opened up a fast lane: Direct flights now connect Nairobi and Hong Kong. Tons of trinkets from the Far East are flooding the African markets. Every few weeks, a new bevy of African kleptocrats heads off on a pilgrimage to Beijing: delegations dispatched by bankrupt countries that are now even denied development aid.

African leaders are prepared to sell out the continent's vast natural resources—recalling the darkest age of European imperialism.

Barred from Britain

Recently, Kenyan President Mwai Kibaki toured the Far Eastern empire in an attempt to shore up the battered self-confidence of his corrupt government. Germany has already frozen €5 million [5 million Euros] in aid pending government action on key corruption cases. Its ambassador in Nairobi is threatening further sanctions, because donations were used "illegally and wastefully" for propaganda purposes.

And the United Kingdom recently revoked a visa issued to Kenya's transport minister, Christopher Ndarathi Murungaru, and barred him—on grounds of corruption—from setting foot on British soil.

During his five-day stint in Beijing, however, Kibaki met with cordial treatment—and graciously accepted his host's pledge of $34 million. The leader was able to "return home a contented man" from a "fruitful visit," according to the pro-government Kenyan newspaper *Daily Nation*. But the critical *Standard* was less euphoric in its assessment of Kibaki's fund-raising trip: "The money is making its way into the government's pockets and bypassing the usual controls," the publication warned. It went on to express the hope that bribes would not induce Kenya's rulers to make "any wild concessions to the Chinese government which they prefer not to disclose at this juncture."

Such fears would appear justified. Zimbabwean President Robert Mugabe was recently welcomed by Chinese President Hu Jintao as a "great friend." While in China, Mugabe reportedly authorized the Chinese to exploit platinum deposits in his ailing country—and received military aircraft worth $100 million in return.

"African leaders like Kenyan President Kibaki or Zimbabwe's dictator Robert Mugabe are making the same mistake made by all African leaders before them," says Kenyan economist James Shikwati, "when they head off on a begging tour to the Far East." The accord with China's power brokers could quickly turn into a pact with the devil. When it comes to alms, African leaders are prepared to sell out the continent's vast natural resources—recalling the darkest age of European imperialism, when entire countries changed hands for glass beads, liquor and copper wire.

Africa's Oil Is Creating New Military Issues for the United States

Christopher Thompson

Christopher Thompson is a contributing writer for the New Statesman.

The Pentagon is to reorganise its military command structure in response to growing fears that the United States is seriously ill-equipped to fight the war against terrorism in Africa. It is a dramatic move, and an admission that the US must reshape its whole military policy if it is to maintain control of Africa for the duration of what Donald Rumsfeld has called "the long war". Suddenly the world's most neglected continent is assuming an increasing global importance as the international oil industry begins to exploit more and more of the west coast of Africa's abundant reserves.

Africom Emerges

The Pentagon at present has five geographic Unified Combatant Commands around the world, and responsibility for Africa is awkwardly divided among three of these. Most of Africa—a batch of 43 countries—falls under the European Command (Eucom), with the remainder divided between the Pacific Command and Central Command (which also runs the wars in Iraq and Afghanistan). Now the Pentagon—under the Joint Chiefs of Staff and the defence department—is working on formal proposals for a unified military command for the continent under the name "Africom".

This significant shift in US relations with Africa comes in the face of myriad threats: fierce economic competition from

Christopher Thompson, "The Scramble for Africa's Oil," *New Statesman*, June 14, 2007. Copyright © 2007 New Statesman, Ltd. Reproduced by permission. www.newstatesman.com/global-issues/2007/06/africa-oil-pentagon-military.

Asia; increasing resource nationalism in Russia and South America; and instability in the Middle East that threatens to spill over into Africa.

The Pentagon hopes to finalise Africom's structure, location and budget this year [2007]. The expectation is that it can break free from Eucom and become operative by mid-2008.

America's new Africa strategy reflects its key priorities in the Middle East: oil and counter-terrorism.

"The break from Europe will occur before 30 September 2008," Professor Peter Pham, a US adviser on Africa to the Pentagon told the *New Statesman*. "The independent command should be up and running by this time next year."

A Pentagon source says the new command, which was originally given the green light by the controversial former US defence secretary Donald Rumsfeld, is likely to be led by William "Kip" Ward, the US army's only four-star African-American general. In 2005, Ward was appointed the US security envoy to the Middle East and he is reportedly close to President George W Bush. He also has boots-on-the-ground experience in Africa: he was a commander during Bill Clinton's ill-fated mission in Somalia in 1993 and he served as a military representative in Egypt in 1998. Ward is now the deputy head of Eucom.

New Terrorism Challenges

America's new Africa strategy reflects its key priorities in the Middle East: oil and counter-terrorism. Currently, the US has in place the loosely defined Trans-Sahara Counter-Terrorism Initiative, incorporating an offshoot of Operation Enduring Freedom that is intended to keep terrorist networks out of the vast, unguarded Sahel. But the lack of a coherent and unified policy on Africa is, according to some observers, hampering

America's efforts in the Middle East. US military sources estimate that up to a quarter of all foreign fighters in Iraq are from Africa, mostly from Algeria and Morocco.

Moreover, there is increasing alarm within the US defence establishment at the creeping "radicalisation" of Africa's Muslims, helped along by the export of hardline, Wahhabi-style clerics from the Arabian peninsula.

"The terrorist challenge [has] increased in Africa in the past year—it's gotten a new lease on life," according to Pham.

But it is the west's increasing dependency on African oil that gives particular urgency to these new directions in the fight against terrorism. Africa's enormous, and largely untapped, reserves are already more important to the west than most Americans recognise.

Increasing Dependence on African Oil

In March 2006, speaking before the Senate armed services committee, General James Jones, the then head of Eucom, said: "Africa currently provides over 15 per cent of US oil imports, and recent explorations in the Gulf of Guinea region indicate potential reserves that could account for 25–35 per cent of US imports within the next decade."

The reality is that a bullish China is willing to offer billions in soft loans and infrastructure projects—all with no strings attached—to secure lucrative acreage.

These high-quality reserves—West African oil is typically low in sulphur and thus ideal for refining—are easily accessible by sea to western Europe and the US. In 2005, the US imported more oil from the Gulf of Guinea than it did from Saudi Arabia and Kuwait combined. Within the next ten years it will import more oil from Africa than from the entire Middle East. Western oil giants such as ExxonMobil, Chevron,

France's Total and Britain's BP and Shell plan to invest tens of billions of dollars in sub-Saharan Africa (far in excess of "aid" inflows to the region).

But though the Gulf of Guinea is one of the few parts of the world where oil production is poised to increase exponentially in the near future, it is also one of the most unstable. In the big three producer countries, Nigeria, Equatorial Guinea and Angola, oil wealth has been a curse for many, enriching political elites at the expense of impoverished citizens. Angola is now China's main supplier of crude oil, supplanting Saudi Arabia last year. The Chinese, along with the rest of oil-hungry Asia, are looking covetously at the entire region's reserves.

A New Cold War?

Looming over West Africa is the spectre of the southern Niger Delta area, which accounts for most of Nigeria's 2.4 million barrels a day. Conflict here offers a taste of what could afflict all of sub-Saharan Africa's oilfields. Since 2003, the Delta has become a virtual war zone as heavily armed rival gangs—with names such as the Black Axes and Vikings—battle for access to pipelines and demand a bigger cut of the petrodollar.

Oil theft, known as "bunkering", costs Nigeria some $4bn (£2.05bn) a year, while foreign companies have been forced to scale back production after kidnappings by Delta militants. Such uncertainties help send world oil prices sky-high.

The Pentagon's new Africa policy is to include a "substantial" humanitarian component, aimed partly at minimising unrest and crime. But the reality is that a bullish China is willing to offer billions in soft loans and infrastructure projects—all with no strings attached—to secure lucrative acreage.

"It's like going back to a Cold War era of politics where the US backs one political faction because their political profile suits their requirements," says Patrick Smith, editor of the newsletter *Africa Confidential,* widely read in policy circles. "It's a move away from criteria of good governance to what is diplomatically convenient."

According to Nicholas Shaxson, author of *Poisoned Wells: the Dirty Politics of African Oil,* "[Africom] comes in the context of a growing conflict with China over our oil supplies."

Increased Military Presence

Africom will significantly increase the US military presence on the continent. At present, the US has 1,500 troops stationed in Africa, principally at its military base in Djibouti, in the eastern horn. That could well double, according to Pham. The US is already conducting naval exercises off the Gulf of Guinea, in part with the intention of stopping Delta insurgents reaching offshore oil rigs. It also plans to beef up the military capacity of African governments to handle their dissidents, with additional "rapid-reaction" US forces available if needed. But—echoing charges levelled at US allies elsewhere in the "war on terror"—there are fears that the many authoritarian governments in sub-Saharan Africa might use such units to crack down on internal dissent.

The Pentagon is hoping that Africom will signal a more constructive foreign policy in the region and a break with the past.

The increased US military presence is already apparent across the Red Sea from Iraq, where, in concert with Ethiopia, Washington has quietly opened up another front in its war on terror. The target: the Somalia-based Islamists whom the Americans claim were responsible for the 1998 bombings of US embassies in Kenya and Tanzania. Earlier this year, US special forces used air strikes against suspected al-Qaeda militants, killing scores.

FBI interrogators have also been dispatched to Ethiopian jails, where hundreds of terror suspects—including Britons—have been held incommunicado since Ethiopia's invasion of Somalia in December last year, according to Human Rights Watch. The problem with this more confrontational approach in Africa is apparent. "There's definitely a danger of the US [being] seen as an imperial exploiter," says Shaxson. "The military presence will raise hackles in certain countries—America will have to tread lightly."

Nonetheless, the Pentagon is hoping that Africom will signal a more constructive foreign policy in the region and a break with the past. "Politically [Africa] is important and that's going to increase in coming years," says Pham. "It's whether the US can sustain the initiative."

Organizations to Contact

The editors have compiled the following list of organizations concerned with the issues debated in this book. The descriptions are derived from materials provided by the organizations. All have publications or information available for interested readers. The list was compiled on the date of publication of the present volume; the information provided here may change. Readers need to remember that many organizations take several weeks or longer to respond to inquiries.

Africa Action
1634 Eye St. NW, #810, Washington, DC   20006
(202) 546-7961 • fax: (202) 546-1545
e-mail: africaaction@igc.org
Web site: www.africaaction.org/

Africa Action is the oldest organization in the United States working on African affairs. Its mission is to change U.S.-African relations to promote political, economic, and social justice in Africa. Its Web site contains a wealth of information about Africa, including a map of Africa; reports on AIDS, Darfur, and economic issues; and resources on key countries.

Africa Faith and Justice Network (AFJN)
PO Box 29378, Washington, DC   20017
(202) 832-3412
e-mail: afjn@afjn.org
Web site: www.acad.cua.edu/afjn

The AFJN comprises religious groups concerned with oppression and injustice in Africa. It analyzes how U.S. foreign policy affects Africa and challenges policies it believes are detrimental to Africans. The network publishes the bimonthly *Around Africa* newsletter, *Action Alerts*, and quarterly documentation pamphlets.

Africa Institute of South Africa (AISA)
PO Box 630, Pretoria   0001
   South Africa
(012) 304 9700
Web site: http://host.yoursoftdns5.com/˜aiorgz/

The Africa Institute of South Africa was established in 1960 to promote research and training on African affairs. AISA funds field research throughout the African continent, conducts community outreach programs, and provides resources to underprivileged schools in rural South Africa. AISA'S Web site includes a reference library and a map and newspaper collection, and it publishes the quarterly *Africa Insight*, as well as a number of other publications.

African Studies Association (ASA)
Rutgers University, 132 George St.
New Brunswick, NJ   08901-1400
(732) 932-8173 • fax: (732) 932-3394
Web site: www.africanstudies.org

The African Studies Association was founded in 1957 as a nonprofit organization open to all individuals and institutions interested in African affairs. Its mission is to bring together people with a scholarly and professional interest in Africa. The ASA also provides information and support services to the African community. It currently produces three publications annually: *ASA News, African Studies Review,* and *History in Africa.*

African Union
PO Box 3243, Addis Ababa
   Ethiopia
(251) 11 551 77 00 • fax: (251) 11 551 78 44
e-mail: konareao@africa-union.org
Web site: www.africa-union.org

The African Union was formed in 1999 by the Organization of African Unity to expedite the process of economic and political integration on the continent. Its Web site includes links to a number of organizations relevant to African economic development.

AllAfrica Global Media
920 M St. SE, Washington, DC   20003
(202) 546-0777 • fax (202) 546-0676
Web site: http://allafrica.com/

AllAfrica Global Media is a multimedia content service provider, systems technology developer, and the largest electronic distributor of African news and information worldwide. Its Web site is among the Internet's largest content sites, posting over a thousand stories daily and offering nearly a million articles in a searchable archive.

Association of Concerned Africa Scholars (ACAS)
Anthropology Department, University of California
Irvine, CA   92697-5100
(949) 824-9652 • fax: (949) 824-4717
e-mail: chair@concernedafricascholars.org
Web site: http://concernedafricascholars.org/

Founded in 1979, the Association of Concerned Africa Scholars is a group of scholars and students of Africa dedicated to formulating alternative analyses of Africa and U.S. government policy, developing communication and action networks among the peoples and scholars of Africa and the United States, and mobilizing support in the United States on critical, current issues related to Africa. The ACAS publishes a newsletter, the *ACAS Bulletin*, and its Web site contains various news updates about Africa.

Brookings Institution
1775 Massachusetts Ave. NW, Washington, DC   20036
(202) 797-6000 • fax: (202) 797-6004
e-mail: brookinfo@brook.edu
Web site: www.brookings.org

The Brookings Institution is a think-tank that conducts research and education in the areas of foreign policy, economics, government, and the social sciences. Its Web site features numerous briefings and publications on the global economy, including several on Africa. Examples include *Africa's Strategic Importance to the U.S.*, and *Are the Millenium Development Goals Unfair to Africa?*

Commission for Africa

Department for International Development
Abercrombie House, Glasgow   G75 8EA
    United Kingdom
(44) 1355 84 3132 • fax: (44) 1355 84 3632
e-mail: enquiry@dfid.gov.uk
Web site: www.commissionforafrica.org/english/home/
newsstories.html

The Commission for Africa was launched by former British prime minister Tony Blair in February 2004 to take a fresh look at Africa's past and present and the international community's role in its development path. The commission produced a report in 2005, available on its Web site. The site also provides various materials that can be used by schools and teachers to explore issues relating to Africa.

Earth Island Institute

300 Broadway, Ste. 28, San Francisco, CA   94133
(415) 788-3666 • fax: (415) 788-7324
e-mail: earthisland@earthisland.org
Web site: www.earthisland.org

Earth Island Institute addresses environmental issues and their relation to such concerns as human rights and economic development in the Third World. The institute's publications include the quarterly *Earth Island Journal*. A search of its Web site also reveals numerous articles and publications on Africa.

Friends of the Earth International

PO Box 19199, 1000 gd Amsterdam
    The Netherlands
(31) 20 622 1369 • fax: (31) 20 639
e-mail: foe@foei.org
Web site: www.foei.org/

Friends of the Earth International is an advocacy organization dedicated to protecting the planet from environmental degradation; preserving biological, cultural, and ethnic diversity; and empowering citizens to have an influential voice in decisions affecting the quality of their environment. It has a U.S. chapter and a Canadian chapter and publishes numerous publications dealing with the environment. Recent publications include "How the World Bank's Energy Framework Sells the Climate and Poor People Short" and "The Tyranny of Free Trade."

Global Policy Forum (GPF)
777 UN Plaza, Ste. 7G, New York, NY   10017
(212) 557-3161 • fax: (212) 557-3165
e-mail: globalpolicy@globalpolicy.org
Web site: www.globalpolicy.org

Global Policy Forum monitors policy making at the United Nations, promotes accountability of global decisions, educates and mobilizes citizen participation, and advocates on vital issues of international peace and justice. The forum publishes policy papers and the *GPF Newsletter*. On its Web site, GPF has a section called "Poverty and Development in Africa" containing numerous articles, speeches, reports, and papers that examine the issues and problems of Africa's development.

Global Trade Watch (GTW)
215 Pennsylvania Ave. SE, Washington, DC   20003
(202) 546-4996
Web site: www.tradewatch.org

Global Trade Watch promotes democracy by challenging corporate globalization, arguing that the current globalization model is neither a random inevitability nor "free trade." GTW works on an array of globalization issues, including health and safety, environmental protection, economic justice, democracy, and accountable governance. It publishes the book *Whose Trade Organization? A Comprehensive Guide to the WTO*, and fact sheets and articles such as "Our World Is Not for Sale" are available on its Web site.

International Monetary Fund (IMF)
700 Nineteenth St. NW, Washington, DC   20431
(202) 623-7000 • fax: (202) 623-4661
e-mail: publicaffairs@imf.org
Web site: www.imf.org

The International Monetary Fund is an international organization of 184 member countries. It was established to promote international monetary cooperation, exchange stability, and orderly exchange arrangements. IMF fosters economic growth and high levels of employment and provides temporary financial assistance to countries. It publishes the quarterly *Finance & Development* and reports on its activities, including the quarterly "Global Financial Stability Report," recent issues of which are available on its Web site along with data on IMF finances and individual country reports.

Oxfam International
226 Causeway St., 5th Fl., Boston, MA   02114-2206
(617) 482-1211 • fax: (617) 728-2594
e-mail: info@oxfamamerica.org
Web site: www.oxfam.org/

Oxfam International is a charitable organization that seeks to provide for the ongoing and emergency needs of people in the world's poorest countries, including many on the African continent. Oxfam is also involved in advocating for more fair trade agreements and other political issues. Its Web site contains a special section on the crisis in Darfur and numerous articles on other issues relevant to Africa.

Save The Children
54 Wilton Rd., Westport, CT   06880
(203) 221-4030
e-mail: twebster@savethechildren.org
Web site: www.savethechildren.org/

Save the Children is an independent aid organization whose mission is to create real and lasting change for children in need in the United States and around the world. It has operations all over Africa, including Sudan, and it concerns itself with providing food, shelter, health care, protection, and recreation for children. Its Web site describes the organization's aid efforts in Africa.

United Nations Conference on Trade and Development (UNCTAD)
Palais des Nations, 1211 Geneva 10
  Switzerland
(41) 22 917 5809 • fax: (41) 22 917 0051
e-mail: info@unctad.org
Web site: www.unctad.org/

UNCTAD was established by the United Nations to help integrate developing countries into the world economy. UNCTAD has organized three UN conferences on least-developed countries, and its Special Programme for Least Developed, Landlocked and Island Developing Countries promotes the socioeconomic development of these countries through research, policy analysis, and technical assistance. Its Web site contains information about the least-developed countries and links to UN reports and other materials relating to trade issues and development.

United Nations Development Programme (UNDP)
1 United Nations Plaza, New York, NY   10017
(212) 906-5315 • fax: (212) 906-5364
Web site: www.undp.org

UNDP funds six thousand projects in more than 150 developing countries and territories. It works with governments, UN agencies, and nongovernmental organizations to enhance self-reliance and promote sustainable human development. Its priorities include improving living standards, protecting the environment, and applying technology to meet human needs. UNDP's publications include the weekly newsletter *UNDP-Flash*, the human development magazine *Choices*, and the annual *UNDP Human Development Report*. On its Web site, UNDP publishes the *Millennium Development Goals*, its annual report, regional data and analysis, speeches and statements, and recent issues of its publications.

United Nations Education, Scientific and Cultural Organization (UNESCO)

7 place de Fontenoy, 75352 Paris 07 SP   France
(33) 1 45 68 10 00 • fax: (33) 1 45 67 16 90
e-mail: bpi@unesco.org
Web site: www.unesco.org

UNESCO is a specialized agency of the United Nations that seeks to promote cooperation among member countries in the areas of education, science, culture, and communication. UNESCO is actively pursuing the UN's Millennium Development Goals, which seek to halve the proportion of people living in extreme poverty in developing countries, achieve universal primary education in all countries, eliminate gender disparity in primary and secondary education, help countries implement a national strategy for sustainable development, and reverse current trends in the loss of environmental resources, all by 2015.

United States African Development Foundation (ADF)

1400 Eye St. NW, Ste. 1000, Washington, DC   20005-2248
(202) 673 3916 • fax: (202) 673-3810
e-mail: info@adf.gov
Website: www.adf.gov/

The African Development Foundation is a federal agency established by the U.S. Congress to promote broad-based, sustainable development in sub-Saharan Africa. ADF has funded more than thirteen hundred projects since 1993. The ADF maintains a local office, staffed with African professionals, in each of the countries in which it operates. Its Web site contains information about the foundation's programs as well as reports and testimony to Congress.

U.S. Agency for International Development (USAID)

1300 Pennsylvania Ave. NW, Washington, DC   20523
(202) 712-4810
Web site: www.usaid.gov

USAID is an independent governmental agency that provides assistance around the world in matters of economic development, global health, and humanitarian assistance. Begun in the period after World War II and the reconstruction of Europe, USAID is active worldwide. Activities in Africa are focused on education, health services (including AIDS/HIV prevention), agricultural development, conflict resolution, conservation, and promoting trade and investment.

World Bank
1818 H St. NW, Washington, DC   20433
(202) 477-1234 • fax: (202) 577-0565
Web site: www.worldbank.org

World Bank seeks to reduce poverty and improve the standards of living of poor people around the world. It promotes sustainable growth and investments in developing countries through loans, technical assistance, and policy guidance. The World Bank Web site contains a section on Africa that offers a variety of publications and resources on Africa and efforts to aid the continent.

World Health Organization (WHO)
Avenue Appia 20, 1211 Geneva 27
    Switzerland
(41) 22 791 21 11 • fax: (41) 22 791 3111
e-mail: info@who.int
Web site: www.who.int

The World Health Organization is the United Nations specialized agency for health. Established in 1948, WHO seeks to promote the highest possible level of health for all people. Health is defined in WHO's constitution as a state of complete physical, mental, and social well-being and not merely the absence of disease or infirmity. WHO is governed by 193 member countries through the World Health Assembly. WHO's Web site contains a library of WHO reports and publications, as well as links to various world health journals and reports.

World Trade Organization (WTO)

Centre William Rappard, CH-1211 Geneva 21
  Switzerland
(41) 22 739 51 11 • fax: (41) 22 731 42 06
e-mail: enquiries@wto.org
Web site: www.wto.org

WTO is a global organization that establishes rules dealing with trade among nations. Two WTO agreements have been negotiated and signed by the bulk of the world's trading nations and ratified in their legislatures. The goal of these agreements is to help producers of goods and services, exporters, and importers conduct their business. WTO publishes trade statistics, research and analysis, studies, reports, and the journal *World Trade Review*. Recent publications are available on the WTO Web site.

Bibliography

Books

Chris Alden	*China in Africa: Partner, Competitor or Hegemon?* London: Zed, 2007.
George B.N. Ayittey	*Africa Unchained: The Blueprint for Africa's Future.* Hampshire, UK: Palgrave Macmillan, 2006.
Harry G. Broadman	*Africa's Silk Road: China and India's New Economic Frontier.* New York: World Bank, 2007.
Patrick Burnett and Firoze Manji, eds.	*From the Slave Trade to 'Free' Trade: How Trade Undermines Democracy and Justice in Africa.* Oxford: Fahamu, 2007.
Robert Calderisi	*The Trouble with Africa: Why Foreign Aid Isn't Working.* Hampshire, UK: Palgrave Macmillan, 2007.
Paul Collier	*The Bottom Billion: Why the Poorest Countries Are Failing and What Can Be Done About It.* Oxford: Oxford University Press, 2007.
Pitou van Dijck and Gerr London	*Developing Countries and the Doha Development Agenda of the WTO.* New York: Routledge, 2006.
William Easterly	*The White Man's Burden: Why the West's Efforts to Aid the Rest Have Done So Much Ill and So Little Good.* New York: Penguin, 2006.

Howard W. French	*A Continent for the Taking: The Tragedy and Hope of Africa.* New York: Vintage, 2005.
John Ghazvinian	*Untapped: The Scramble for Africa's Oil.* Orlando, FL: Harcourt, 2007.
Sanjeev Gupta, Ulrich Jacoby, and Kevin Carey	*Sub-Saharan Africa: Forging New Trade Links with Asia.* Washington, DC: International Monetary Fund, 2007.
Kempe Ronald Hope	*Poverty, Livelihoods, and Governance in Africa: Fulfilling the Development Promise.* Hampshire, UK: Palgrave Macmillan, 2008.
Marcel Kitissou	*Africa in China's Global Strategy.* London: Adonis & Abbey, 2007.
Princeton N. Lyman and Patricia Dorff, eds.	*Beyond Humanitarianism: What You Need to Know About Africa and Why It Matters.* Washington, DC: Brookings, 2008.
Alex F. McCalla and John Nash, eds.	*Reforming Agricultural Trade for Developing Countries.* Washington, DC: World Bank, 2007.
Martin Meredith	*The Fate of Africa: A History of Fifty Years of Independence.* New York: PublicAffairs, 2006.
Chamberlain S. Peterside	*Wealth Effect: Africa in Midst of Global Economic Transformation.* Morrisville, NC: Lulu, 2007.

| Jeffrey Sachs | *The End of Poverty: Economic Possibilities for Our Time.* New York: Penguin, 2005. |
| Daniel K. Song'ony | *Economic Development in Africa in the Age of Globalization and HIV/AIDS.* Bloomington, IN: Authorhouse, 2008. |

Periodicals

Chicago-Tribune	"A Tank of Gas, a World of Trouble," April 15, 2008. www.chicagotribune.com/topic/chi-oil-email,1,4338993.story?page=9.
Bruce Dixon	"Africa—Where the Next US Oil Wars Will Be," *Black Agenda Report,* February 28, 2007. www.blackagendareport.com/index.php?option=com_content&task=view&id=114.
Paul Drain	"Africa's Devastating Challenge: HIV/AIDS and Extreme Poverty," *Seattle Post-Intelligencer,* August 6, 2006. http://seattlepi.nwsource.com/opinion/280140_focus06.html.
Daniel Flynn	"African Nations Should Nationalise Oil: Venezuela," *Global Research,* April 12, 2008. http://globalresearch.ca/index.php?context=va&aid=8663.
Global Agenda	"Whatever It Takes; Report on Global Poverty; Sachs's Solutions," January 18, 2005.

Edward Harris   "Oil Boom, Shifting Politics Give
Africa Best Chance in Decades," *New
York Times*, April 3, 2007. http://
nytimes.com/articles/2007/07/01/
business/business/doc42e748a6d672e
65886257309004bdedf.txt.

Andrew Leonard   "How the World Works: Blood for
Oil in the Horn of Africa," *Salon*,
April 24, 2007. www.salon.com/tech/
htww/2007/04/24/ogaden/.

Abraham   "Can Africa Solve African Problems?"
McLaughlin   *Christian Science Monitor*, January 4,
2005. www.csmonitor.com/2005/0104/
p07s01-woaf.html.

Abu Muse   "Africa Needs More Foreign Aid—
UN," *Guardian*, July 23, 2007.
www.ippmedia.com/ipp/guardian/
2007/07/23/94960.html.

New York Times   "Africa's Chance," November 2, 2007.
www.nytimes.com/2007/11/02/
opinion/02fri1.html?_r=2&oref=
slogin&oref=slogin.

OECD Observer   "Africa's Economy: Aid and Growth,"
No. 249, May 2005.
www.oecdobserver.org/news/fullstory.
php/aid/1618/Africa%92s_economy:
_Aid_and_growth_.html.

Alexis Okeowo   "Is Global Warming Drowning Africa?" *Time*, September 21, 2007.
www.time.com/time/world/article/
0,8599,1664429,00.html.

Alex Perry	"Africa's Oil Dreams," *Time*, May 31, 2007. www.time.com/time/magazine/article/0,9171,1626751-2,00.html.
Robert B. Reich	"A Case for Tailoring—and Slowing—Free Trade in Poor Nations," *New York Times*, March 31, 2006.
Jeffrey Sachs	"Beware False Tradeoffs," *Foreign Affairs*, January 23, 2007. http://www.foreignaffairs.org/special/global_health/sachs.
Slate	"Does Africa Measure Up to the Hype?" April 3, 2007. http://www.slate.com/id/2163389/entry/2163395/.
Marian L. Tupy and Christopher Preble	"Trade, Not Aid," *Reason Online*, June 17, 2005. www.reason.com/news/show/32936.html.

Internet Sources

BBC News	"What Are the Challenges Facing Africa?" May 7, 2004. http://news.bbc.co.uk/2/hi/talking_point/3682523.stm.
Clare Nullis	"Africa Faces Growing Obesity Problem," Associated Press, November 29, 2006. www.breitbart.com/article.php?id=D8LN0P6G1&show_article=1.
Steve Schifferes	"Why Can't Africa Tackle Poverty?" BBC News, September 27, 2007. http://news.bbc.co.uk/2/hi/business/7013764.stm.

Brian Smith   "China's Growing Trade with Africa Indicative of Sino-Western Energy Conflicts," World Socialist Web Site, January 24, 2006. www.wsws.org/articles/2006/jan2006/chin-j24.shtml.

Chris Tomlinson   "Much Aid to Africa on Road to Nowhere," Associated Press, December 20, 2007. www.wtopnews.com/?nid=387&sid=1313797.

Index